C# Fundamentals: The Complete Beginner's Guide to C# 13 and .NET 9

Adam Seebeck

United States

C# Fundamentals: The Complete Beginner's Guide to C# 13 and .NET 9

Author: Adam Seebeck

Copy Editor: Samantha Seebeck

For permission to use material from this book, please contact:
http://www.unqbd.com/Contact
or email: PermissionRequest@unQbd.com

Hardcover ISBN: 978-1-954086-44-9
Paperback ISBN: 978-1-954086-43-2

Edition: 7.01

unQbd
581 N Park Ave #4201
Apopka, FL 32704
USA

Print Year: 2024

Unless otherwise noted, all items © unQbd.

unQbd (pronounced "un-cubed") is a streaming service that offers a variety of books that can be read on your choice of internet-connected device. You can read as much as you want for one low yearly price. unQbd books are also available for purchase in print form.

Unlimited books, audio books, and more.

Membership Benefits

Your **FREE**, 7-day trial comes with:

Unlimited Access

✅ Get **FULL** and **UNLIMITED** access to our entire collection of books and audiobooks. No limits, no restrictions, just endless reading and listening.

Community Access

✅ Connect with fellow **BOOK LOVERS** and **AUTHORS**. Ask questions directly from interactive books, share your thoughts, and communicate in our Community Access area. Socialize, learn, and deepen your love of reading!

Start your membership today at unQbd.com

TABLE OF CONTENTS

ABOUT THIS BOOK

Written by a seasoned higher education instructor, *C# Fundamentals* is more than just a book—it's a journey through the essentials of software development, structured as an interactive course. With engaging activities, quizzes, and easy-to-follow examples, this book is your companion in mastering the core concepts of software development using the C# language.

Here are some of the unique teaching techniques employed in this book to ensure a comprehensive learning experience:

➢ **Quick Reference Essentials:** Each section kicks off with a succinct explanation accompanied by code snippets to quickly get you acquainted with the topic at hand.

➢ **Full Examples:** Building upon the Quick Reference Essentials, these sections present real-world examples to deepen your understanding. Whether it's creating a simple calculator or a basic web application, you'll see the concepts in action.

➢ **Walkthroughs:** These are your step-by-step guides to completing specific tasks, you will be provided with all the information needed to create fully functional applications from scratch.

➢ **Activities:** Put what you've learned to the test with a range of assignments that reinforce the concepts discussed in each section.

➢ **Mini Quizzes:** A quick checkpoint to gauge your comprehension and reinforce your understanding of the material.

Delve into software development using the **C#** language along with the user-friendly and accessible **Visual Studio** software (free to download). Whether you're a seasoned developer or a complete novice, this book has something to offer. With flowcharts, screenshots, and additional visual aids employed throughout, complex concepts are broken down into digestible chunks.

C# Fundamentals is your go-to resource, blending theory with practical applications to provide a robust learning experience.

INTRODUCTION TO C#

C# (pronounced "C Sharp") is a modern, user-friendly, **object-oriented** programming language developed by Microsoft Corporation. Since its inception in 2002, C# has undergone several iterations, with the latest version, 13.0, making its debut in November 2024. It remains the language of choice within Microsoft's esteemed Visual Studio platform, a comprehensive **Integrated Development Environment** (IDE) dedicated to application development.

At the core of C# lies the **.NET platform**, which **.NET 9** now embodies, encompassing a robust set of components crucial for running modern applications. A key component, the **Common Language Runtime** (CLR), orchestrates the execution of code written in a language that complies with the **Common Language Infrastructure** (CLI), such as C#. Initially, the code is compiled into an **intermediate language** (IL). The CLR's Just-In-Time (JIT) compiler then translates the IL code into native machine code (binary) at the point of execution, enabling seamless computer comprehension.

The .NET platform, with its .NET 9 iteration, contains numerous shared class libraries that simplify the development process. Instead of starting from scratch, developers can leverage these pre-built libraries for common tasks. For example, reading data from a text file becomes straightforward with built-in classes like *StreamReader* or methods such as *File.ReadAllText*, eliminating the need for manual recreation.

One of the defining features of C# is its versatility. As a general-purpose language, C# is engineered to tackle a broad spectrum of applications—from web development to desktop, mobile apps, and even gaming.

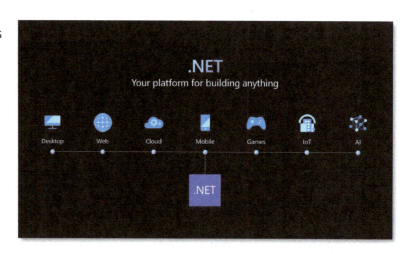

Image Source: https://devblogs.microsoft.com/dotnet/wp-content/uploads/sites/10/2022/11/dotnet-platform2.png

What's new in C# 13? In this version, C# 13 and .NET 9 introduce several exciting enhancements that make coding simpler and more powerful. If you are new to C#, you may want to skip this section about what's new in C# 13 and the next one on .NET 9. The information below highlights key new features, which will be covered in detail later in this book.

Expanded Pattern Matching: C# 13 introduces new pattern matching capabilities, such as **list patterns** and **relational patterns**, which allow for more concise and expressive code when working with complex data structures. These patterns simplify conditional logic by allowing you to easily match data within collections.

Example: Expanded Pattern Matching

```csharp
if (myList is [1, 2, .., 10])
{
        Console.WriteLine("The list starts with 1 and 2 and ends with 10.");
}
```

Primary Constructors for Classes: C# 13 introduces primary constructors for non-record classes. This allows parameters to be added directly in the class declaration, which simplifies initialization logic.

Example: Primary Constructors for Classes

```csharp
public class Product(int id, string name)
{
        public int Id { get; } = id;
        public string Name { get; } = name;
}
```

File-Scoped Types: You can now define types that are restricted to a specific file. This is useful for scoping certain utility classes that should not be available throughout the entire project.

Improvements to Interpolated Strings: C# 13 makes working with interpolated strings easier. You can now use string interpolation in more flexible ways, even across multiple lines without explicit concatenation.

Enhanced Lambda Expressions: Lambda expressions in C# 13 now support more complex patterns, allowing you to write concise and expressive function-like code without the overhead of defining a separate method.

What's New in .NET 9? .NET 9 brings numerous changes and improvements that help make application development smoother and more efficient:

- **New ASP.NET Core Features**: .NET 9 improves ASP.NET Core with enhanced performance and updated middleware features. These features are especially useful for building cloud-native, microservice architectures.

- **AOT Compilation**: .NET 9 introduces **Ahead-of-Time (AOT)** compilation, which allows certain applications to be compiled directly to native code. This results in faster startup times and reduced memory usage, particularly beneficial for cloud and mobile applications.

- **Improved Diagnostics and Observability**: Enhanced diagnostics and logging capabilities in .NET 9 make it easier to monitor and troubleshoot live applications. New tooling has been integrated to improve support for distributed tracing, allowing developers to better understand system behavior across services.

- **Native ARM Support**: ARM64 support has been further optimized, allowing .NET 9 applications to run more efficiently on devices with ARM processors, like tablets and single-board computers.

- **Unified API Experience**: .NET 9 continues the effort to unify the platform with improvements in APIs. This means better cross-platform consistency when working with features like file handling, networking, and serialization.

Now that you are familiar with the latest features in C# 13 and .NET 9, let's explore the exciting possibilities of what you can create with these powerful tools.

What type of applications can you build with C#? C# 13, coupled with the power of .NET 9, can be used to develop various types of applications:

- **Console Applications:** Console Applications are text-driven and do not include graphical elements such as buttons or images. These are excellent for demonstrating basic C# concepts, which is why this book focuses on text-based examples.

- **Web Applications:** With ASP.NET Core in .NET 9, building scalable and performant web applications has never been easier. Enhanced middleware and better integration with cloud services make it a great choice for developing dynamic websites.

- **Mobile Applications:** Using .NET MAUI, C# 13 allows for rapid development of mobile applications for iOS and Android. Cross-platform development is further simplified with .NET MAUI enhancements, reducing the need for duplicate code.

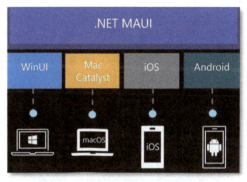

- **Games:** Unity, a widely used game development framework, allows developers to create 2D, 3D, virtual, and mixed-reality games using C# 13. Unity continues to provide an extensive toolset for game development, fully supported by the latest advancements in C#.

- **Desktop Software:** C# 13 and .NET MAUI enable developers to create applications for Windows, macOS, and Linux. Whether it's a business application using WPF or a utility program, C# offers a strong foundation for building interactive user experiences.

VISUAL STUDIO: INSTALLING

Visual Studio can be downloaded from "VisualStudio.Microsoft.com/downloads". Select the Community edition, which is available free of charge.

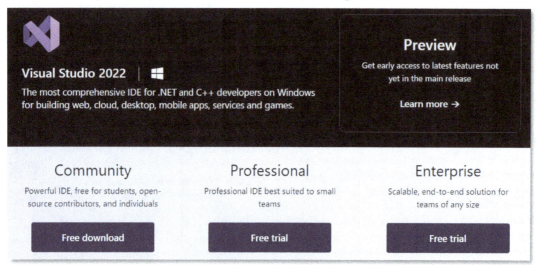

The screen below will be displayed after downloading and beginning the installation process. This interface contains the components available for installation. Components can always be added later by going to the top menu bar and selecting "Tools -> Get Tools and Features".

For the purposes of this book, ensure to have at least ".NET desktop development" component selected. Review all the additional components available to install to become familiar with the options. Click the "Install" or "Modify" button to proceed with the installation.

VISUAL STUDIO: CONSOLE APPLICATION SETUP

The following instructions explain how to create a **Console Application**. Console Applications are great for demonstrating concepts; they are simple text-based applications.

Walkthrough: Microsoft Windows setup for a Console Application ***may vary for Mac computers*

1. Open *Visual Studio* from your Desktop or Start Menu.

2. Click "Create a new project".

3. In the Project types dropdown select "Console" and select "Console App".

4. Click "Next" in the bottom right corner.

5. Give the project a name, select a location to save the project, and then click "Next" in the bottom right corner.

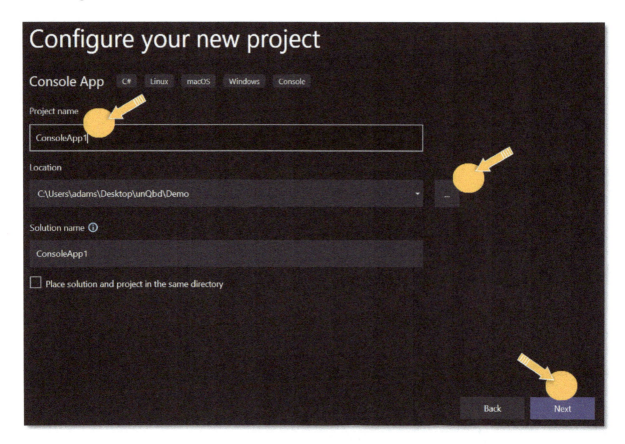

6. Click the "Create" button in the bottom right corner.

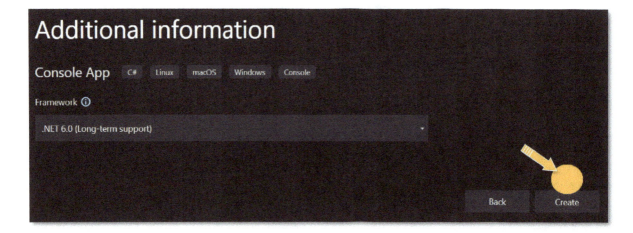

CONSOLE APPLICATION: "HELLO WORLD!"

When learning a new programming language, it is a tradition to display the words "Hello, World!" on the screen. Please note, this is the only example in the book where an explanation is not provided about the coding and simply the instructions are given to produce the results.

Walkthrough: Hello World

1. Create a Console application named *HelloWorld*. The steps to create a Console application can be found in the previous section *"Visual Studio: Console Application Setup"*.

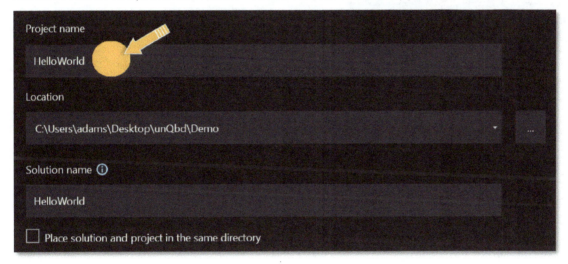

2. By default, Console applications display "Hello, World!" when created. Please note, the file "Program.cs" should automatically load, if it does not double click it from the Solution Explorer menu.

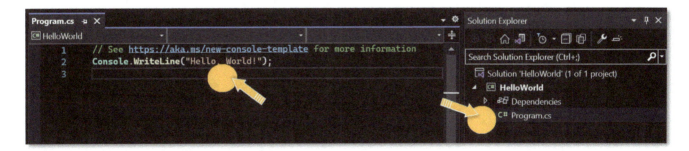

3. Press the play button or the F5 key to run the Console application.

4. The "Hello, World" Console application will load.

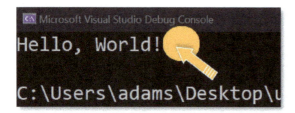

Congratulations on completing your first C# program!

COMMENTS

Program **comments** in C# are annotations within the source code that provide explanations or insights into the code's functionality. They are **non-executing** parts of the code and do not affect program execution. Comments are essential for maintaining code clarity and facilitating teamwork.

There are several types of comments in C#:

- **Line Comments:** Use two forward slashes (//) to comment a single line. The compiler ignores everything from the // to the end of the line.

- **Block Comments:** Enclose multiple lines of code or text within /* and */ to create a block comment. Everything between these markers is treated as a comment.

- **Inline Comments:** These are line comments placed at the end of a line of code, following executable code, to explain the purpose of the specific code segment on that line.

While comments are critical for explaining complex logic or the purpose of code constructs, it is a best practice to write code that is as self-explanatory as possible, using meaningful variable names and clear structure. Comments should ideally explain why certain decisions were made, rather than what the code is doing.

Additionally, developers often use block or line comments to 'comment out' code temporarily during testing or debugging. However, this should be cleaned up before the code is finalized to prevent clutter.

Modern C# IDEs, like Visual Studio, provide convenient features for adding, removing, and managing comments, making it easier for developers to maintain well-documented code.

Example: Line comment

```
// Anything after two forward slashes on this line will not execute.
Console.Write("Hello World!"); // A comment can also be placed after code.
```

Example: Block comment

```
/* Comment out multiple lines of code.
   Anything in this area is also a comment.
*/
```

Visual Studio has a convenient way to quickly comment or uncomment selected lines of code. Click on the Comment or Uncomment buttons.

SNIPPET & SHORTCUT KEYS

Snippets and **shortcut keys** are powerful features in Visual Studio that save time by automating repetitive coding tasks and streamlining the development workflow.

Code Snippets: By typing a keyword and pressing the Tab key twice, a predefined code fragment is inserted into your code. Ensure you're in the correct context for the snippet to work. For example, typing **cw** and pressing Tab twice will produce:

Example: cw (tab) (tab)

```
// cw (tab)(tab) : Type cw and then press the tab key twice, the line below will display
Console.WriteLine();
```

Here are some commonly used snippets and their results:

- **cw** then Tab twice: Inserts **Console.WriteLine();**

- **while** then Tab twice: Creates a **while** loop structure

- **for** then Tab twice: Generates a **for** loop, with placeholders for loop control variables

- **foreach** then Tab twice: Inserts a **foreach** loop, with placeholders for the iterator and collection

- **do** then Tab twice: Produces a **do while** loop structure

- **prop** then Tab twice: Creates an auto-implemented property with public get and set accessors

Shortcut Keys:

- Pressing **F5** starts the debugging session, allowing you to run your code with the debugger attached, stepping through the code, and inspecting variables.

- Pressing **Ctrl+F5** starts the program without the debugger, which can be faster and is used when debugging is not necessary.

Consistent use of these features can significantly reduce the amount of typing required and help maintain focus on more complex tasks.

VARIABLES AND DATA TYPES

A **variable** is a named reference to a memory location that stores data which can be retrieved or modified during program execution. The name of the variable acts as an identifier, while the content it points to the value can change.

Data types are crucial as they define the kind of data a variable can hold and determine the operations that can be performed with that data. For instance, a **string** data type holds text, and an **integer** (int) holds whole numbers.

Declare a variable by specifying the data type followed by the variable name.

Example: Declare a variable

```
string myStringName;
```

Example: Initialize a variable upon declaration

```
string myStringName = "Hello";
```

After a variable is declared, you can change its value without repeating the data type:

Example: Assign a new value

```
myStringName = "Hello again";
```

Numeric data types have specific suffixes to clarify the type of the literal:

Example: Numeric data types

```
int numOne = 5;
float numTwo = 2.55f; // 'f' specifies a float literal
double numThree = 3.33;  // No suffix needed, defaults to double
decimal numFour = 4.66m; // 'm' specifies a decimal literal
```

Using **var** allows the compiler to infer the variable's type based on the assigned value:

Example: var

```
var theWord = "hello"; // Inferred as sting
var theNumber = 5;     // Inferred as int
```

Every data type has an associated memory size and value range. The smallest unit of memory is a **bit**, and there are eight bits in a **byte**. Here's a table of common data types, their memory size, range, and an example:

Data Types	Bytes	Range	Example
byte	1	0 to 255	7
short	2	-32,768 to 32,767	-10
int	4	-2,147,483,648 to 2,147,483,647	12
long	8	-9,233,372,036,854,775,808 to 9,233,373,036,854,775,807	-54
sbyte	1	-128 to 127	5
ushort	2	0 to 65,535	7
uint	4	0 to 4,294,967,295	9
ulong	8	0 to 18,446,744,073,709,551,615	11
float	4	Represents a floating point value up to 7 digits	12.3
double	8	Represents a floating point value up to 16 digits	12.35
decimal	16	Represents a floating point value up to 29 significant digits	12.356
bool	1	Logical Boolean type (can only be True or False)	True
char	2	A single Unicode character	H
string	varies	A sequence of characters	Hello

Data types can be either **signed** or **unsigned**. Signed types, like **int** and **short**, can store both positive and negative numbers, whereas unsigned types, like **uint** and **ushort**, can only store positive values.

The choice of data type is significant and depends on the nature of the data and the required range of values, balancing the precision and memory efficiency of the program.

MINI QUIZ: VARIABLES AND DATA TYPES

Mini Quiz

1. Which of the following is a data type?

    A. 5
    B. Int
    C. "Hello"
    D. Console.ReadLine()

2. What data type is the most memory efficient to use if a number from 1 to 10 needs to be stored?

    A. Int
    B. String
    C. Byte
    D. Char

3. Will the following code compile without errors in C#?

```
int myNumber = "5";
```

    A. Yes
    B. No

4. When declaring a floating-point number in C#, what character needs to be placed after the value to denote it as a float?

    A. M
    B. F
    C. D
    D. A character is not needed

5. Can an unsigned integer type store a negative value such as -21?

    A. Yes
    B. No

Mini Quiz Answers

5. B – Unsigned types cannot be negative

4. B

3. B – Needs to be 5 not "5"

2. C – Bytes have a range from 0 to 255 and will use the smallest amount of memory

1. B

NAMING CONVENTIONS

Proper naming and capitalization in C# enhance code readability and maintainability. The two primary capitalization styles are Camel Casing and Pascal Casing:

- **Camel Casing**: The first letter of the first word is lowercase, subsequent words start with an uppercase letter (e.g., localVariableName).

- **Pascal Casing**: Every word starts with an uppercase letter (e.g., ClassName, MethodName).

Camel Casing is typically used for local variables and method arguments. Pascal Casing is used for classes, methods, properties, and constants. (though constants are often written in all uppercase with underscores, like MAX_SIZE).

Avoid prefixes, as they can make names less clear (e.g., use employeeName instead of strEmployeeName). For fields, especially private ones, camel casing is common (e.g., internalCount). Methods should have verb-based names that reflect their actions, like CalculateTotal.

Acronyms in names follow capitalization rules based on their length: short acronyms remain in uppercase (HTTPError), while longer ones capitalize only the first letter (XmlHttpRequest).

Names should not include hyphens, spaces, non-alphanumeric characters, and should not start with a number. Always aim for **self-documenting** and specific names that make the purpose of the variable or method clear without additional context.

Example: Casing examples

```
int gameScoreTotal; // Camel Case for a local variable

public class GameCalculator { } // Pascal Case for a class name

public void CalculateScore() { } // Pascal Case for a method name

const int MAX_PLAYERS = 5; // Uppercase for constants
```

As you progress through this book, observe the naming conventions used and consider how they contribute to the clarity of the code.

MINI QUIZ: NAMING CONVENTIONS

Mini Quiz

1. Select all the valid Camel Casing names.

      A. response

      B. myResponse

      C. 2ndResponse

      D. userResponse

      E. my-Response

2. Select all the valid Pascal Casing names.

      A. Response

      B. MyResponse

      C. SecondResponse

      D. UserResponse

      E. My_Response

3. Which of the following would NOT be considered a self-documenting name? (Choose all that apply.)

      A. Method1

      B. totalScore

      C. HealthLevel

      D. Calculate1

      E. ProcessUserData

Mini Quiz Answers

1. A, B, D
2. A, B, C, D
3. A, D

OPERATORS

Operators are special symbols in C# that perform operations on operands. They can be categorized by their functionality.

Category	Operator	Description	Example	Result
Arithmetic	+	Addition	5 + 1	6
	-	Subtraction	5 − 1	4
	*	Multiplication	5 * 2	10
	/	Division	5 / 2	2.5
	%	Remainder	5 % 2	1
Assignment	=	Assigns a value	x = 5	x is 5
	+=	Adds and assigns	x += 5	x is x+5
	-=	Subtracts and assigns	x -= 5	x is x-5
Relational	==	Equality	x == 5	true if x is 5
	!=	Inequality	x != 5	true if x is not 5
	<	Less than	x < 5	true if x is less than 5
	>	Greater than	x > 5	true if x is greater than 5
	<=	Less than or equal to	x <= 5	true if x is less than or equal to 5
	>=	Greater than or equal to	x >= 5	true if x is greater than or equal to 5
Increment/Decrement	++	Increments value by 1	x++	x is incremented by 1
	--	Decrements value by 1	x--	x is decremented by 1
String Concatenation	+	Concatenates strings together	"Hi" + " John"	"Hi John"
Conditional	&&	Logical AND	(x == 5) && (y == 6)	true if both conditions are true
	||	Logical OR	(x == 5) || (y == 6)	true if at least one condition is true
Logical Negation	!	Inverts the truth value	!(x == 5)	true if x is not 5
Ternary	?:	Returns one of two values	x > 5 ? "Greater" : "Lesser"	"Greater" if x is greater than 5, "Lesser" otherwise

INPUT & OUTPUT

Console applications are an excellent tool for illustrating computer concepts. They enable simple text **output** and user **input**. This book therefore emphasizes their use.

To output text in a Console application, **Write** and **WriteLine** methods are available:

Example: Output text

```
Console.Write("Hello ");        // Write does not append a new line
Console.Write("World!");        // Output: Hello World!

Console.WriteLine("Hello ");    // WriteLine appends a new line
Console.WriteLine("World!");    // Output: Hello
                                //            World!
```

Below is a brief description of what each part of the above code represents.

```
Console.WriteLine("Hello World!"); // Writes "Hello World!" followed by a newline to the console
```

Console.	WriteLine	(	Hello World!	");
Selects the Console Class (Classes covered in a later section)	Tells the console to output text	"	The text to output on the console	

To receive input, **ReadLine** is used. This method waits for the user to enter text and press "Enter":

Example: Input text

```
Console.ReadLine(); // Waits for user input
```

Example: To store user input in a variable

```
string saveToVariable = Console.ReadLine();
```

Should you need a different data type, conversion is necessary, which will be discussed in the "Parse and TryParse" section.

You can simplify "Console.WriteLine" to **WriteLine** by adding "using static System.Console;" to the top of your Program.cs file. The usage of namespaces and directives will be explained in a subsequent chapter.

Example: WriteLine and ReadLine without using "Console."

```
using static System.Console;" // Enables direct access to static members of Console

WriteLine("No need to prefix with Console."); // Now WriteLine can be used directly
ReadLine();
```

Different techniques for data output are shown below. This includes **string interpolation**, denoted by **$**, which allows embedding variables directly in strings for readability.

Full Example: Variables displayed in multiple ways

```
string todaysDay = "Tuesday";

Console.WriteLine(todaysDay);              // Output: Tuesday
Console.WriteLine("Today is " + todaysDay);   // Output: Today is Tuesday
Console.WriteLine("Today is {0}", todaysDay); // Output: Today is Tuesday
Console.WriteLine($"Today is {todaysDay}");  // Output: Today is Tuesday
```

Escape characters provide a way to include characters in a string that would otherwise be hard to express. For instance, to include quotes inside a string literal, use **\"**.

Example: Escape character for quote

```
Console.WriteLine("Include a quote like this: \"Hello\""); // Output includes quotes around Hello
```

Escape sequences like **\n** for a new line and **\t** for a tab are useful for formatting.

Example: Tab and Newline

```
Console.WriteLine("\tHello\nWorld"); //Outputs Hello with a tab space and World on a new line
```

Use the **@** symbol to create **verbatim string literals**, which ignore escape sequences. This is useful for file paths.

Example: File name with backslashes compared to file name with "@" symbol

```
Console.WriteLine("C:\\Users\\ComputerUser\\Desktop\\AFile.doc"); // Without verbatim literal
Console.WriteLine(@"C:\Users\ComputerUser\Desktop\AFile.doc");    // With verbatim literal
```

Note that verbatim string literals are particularly useful when dealing with Windows file paths due to the backslash being the directory separator.

ACTIVITY: ECHOING USER INPUT

Activity: In this activity, you will create a simple console application that interacts with the user. The goal is to ask the user for their name and then use it in a greeting. This exercise will help you understand how to display information to the user and how to process user input.

Requirements:

1. The application should display the question: "Hello, what is your name?".

2. It should then wait for the user to input their name and press Enter.

3. After the user has entered their name, the application should store the input in a variable.

4. Finally, the application should use this variable to display a personalized thank you message.

Expected Output: When run, the program should behave as follows:

```
Hello, what is your name?

[The user enters their name and presses Enter]

Thank you, [name that was saved].
```

Hints:

- Use **Console.WriteLine** or **Console.Write** for displaying the question.

- Use **Console.ReadLine** to read the user's input.

- A variable of type **string** can store the input from the user.

- String interpolation (**$""**) or concatenation can be used to create the thank you message.

Need additional help with the solution?

https://www.unQbd.com/Solutions/CSharp7th/DisplayUserInput

CASTING

Casting is the conversion from one data type to another and is a common operation in C#. There are two forms of casting: **implicit** and **explicit**.

- **Implicit Casting** is performed by the C# compiler without the need for explicit syntax. This type of casting is safe and automatic when converting a smaller type to a larger type, ensuring no loss of data.

- **Explicit Casting** must be instructed by the programmer when converting a larger type to a smaller one. This acknowledges the risk of data loss due to the narrowing of the type.

When performing arithmetic operations, operands must be of the same type. For example, when a *short* (ranging from -32,768 to 32,767) is added to an *int* (ranging from -2,147,483,648 to 2,147,483,647), the short is automatically cast to an int.

Example: Implicit Casting

```
short num1 = 50;
int num2 = 600;
int sum = num1 + num2; // 'num1' is automatically promoted to 'int'
```

Example: Explicit Casting

```
decimal firstNumber = 50.1234m;
int secondNumber= 2;

// Truncating 'firstNumber' by explicitly casting to 'int'
int sum = (int)firstNumber + secondNumber; // Result is 52, '.1234' is truncated
```

Casting is straightforward when dealing with numeric types such as converting a *short* to an *int*. For converting between non-numeric types, such as from *string* to *int*, the Parse and TryParse methods are more appropriate and are discussed in the "Parse and TryParse" section of this book.

MINI QUIZ: CASTING

Mini Quiz

1. What type of casting is being used in the following example?

```
long firstNumber = 603453;
int secondNumber = 54;
int total = (int)firstNumber + secondNumber;
```

    A. Implicit

    B. Explicit

    C. Will throw an error

2. What type of casting is being used in the following example?

```
byte firstNumber = 60;
int secondNumber = 700;
int total = firstNumber + secondNumber;
```

    A. Implicit

    B. Explicit

    C. Will throw an error

3. What type of casting is being used in the following example?

```
long firstNumber = 12;
int secondNumber = 343;
int sum = firstNumber + secondNumber;
```

    A. Implicit

    B. Explicit

    C. Will throw an error

Mini Quiz Answers

3. C
2. A
1. B

IF, ELSE IF, AND ELSE STATEMENTS

Decision-making is a fundamental aspect of programming. **if**, **else if**, and **else** statements control the flow of execution based on Boolean expressions.

An *'if'* statement executes the enclosed code block only when its condition evaluates to true. Typically, these conditions involve variables, allowing for dynamic decision-making.

Example: 'If' Statement with a Variable

```
string todaysDay = "Monday";

if (todaysDay == "Monday")
{
    // This code executes because the condition is true.
}
```

An *'else'* statement serves as a fallback, executing when the preceding *'if'* condition is false.

Example: 'If' and 'else' Statement

```
string todaysDay = "Tuesday";

if (todaysDay == "Monday")
{
    Console.WriteLine("Today is Monday");
}
else
{
    Console.WriteLine("Today is NOT Monday"); // Output: "Today is NOT Monday"
}
```

'else if' allows for multiple, distinct conditions. Only the first true condition's block will execute, and the rest will be ignored. Order is crucial; the conditions are evaluated top to bottom.

Example: "If" "else if" and "else" Statement

```
string todaysDay = "Tuesday";
if (todaysDay == "Monday")
{
    Console.WriteLine("Today is Monday");
}
else if (todaysDay == "Tuesday")
{
    Console.WriteLine("Today is Tuesday");  // Output: "Today is Tuesday"
}
else if (todaysDay == "Wednesday")
{
    Console.WriteLine("Today is Wednesday");
}
else
{
    Console.WriteLine("Today is NOT Monday, Tuesday, or Wednesday");
}
```

While single-line statements don't require braces, using them is a best practice for clarity. If the statement is exactly one line of code they are not needed. They are only required for multiple lines of code. This book always uses curly brackets (excluding example below).

Example: Using Braces

```
string todaysDay = "Tuesday";

if (todaysDay == "Monday")
    Console.WriteLine("Today is Monday");
else if (todaysDay == "Tuesday")
    Console.WriteLine("Today is Tuesday"); // Output: "Today is Tuesday"
else if (todaysDay == "Wednesday")
{
    // Curly brackets are needed if there are more than 1 statement following a condition
    Console.WriteLine("Today is Wednesday");
    Console.WriteLine("It is the middle of the work week!");
}
else
    Console.WriteLine("Today is NOT Monday, Tuesday, or Wednesday");
```

Nesting *'if'* statements allows for more complex decision trees, where each condition can have its own sub-conditions.

Example: Nested *'if'* Statement

```
bool gameActive = true;
int health = 40;

if (gameActive == true)
{
        Console.WriteLine("Game is Active!");

        if (health == 100) // Nested 'if' Statement
        {
                Console.WriteLine("You are in perfect health!");
        }
        else
        {
                Console.WriteLine("You have been hurt");
        }
}
```

Conditional operators (covered in the "Operators" section) are commonly used in "if" and "else if" statements. In the example below the "&&" operator is used, meaning that both conditions must be true.

Example: Conditional Operators

```
bool gameActive = true;
string player = "Adam";

if (gameActive == true && player == "Adam")
{
        Console.WriteLine("The game is active AND Adam is alive." );
}

if (gameActive == true || player == "Adam")
{
        Console.WriteLine("The game is active OR Adam is Alive!");
}
```

Use conditional operators to create more concise and powerful conditions, enhancing your program's decision-making capabilities.

ACTIVITY: DECISION MAKING BASED ON MOOD

Activity: In this activity, you will create a console application that responds to the user's current mood. Follow these steps to build the application:

1. Prompt the user with the question: "What kind of mood are you in? Good, Ok, or Bad?".

2. Capture and store the user's response in a variable.

3. Use **if**, **else if**, and **else** statements to provide customized responses based on the user's input. Include a catch-all **else** statement for inputs that do not match the expected moods.

Expected Output Example:

If the user types "Good", the output will be:

```
What kind of mood are you in? Good, Ok, or Bad?

Good

Great to hear you're feeling good!
```

Hints:

- Utilize **if**, **else if**, and **else** statements to handle the different possible responses.

- Remember that an **if** statement checks for a specific condition, **else if** checks for additional conditions only if the previous **if** or **else if** conditions weren't met, and **else** covers any situation that wasn't addressed by preceding conditions.

- For string comparisons, use the equality operator **==** to compare the user's input to the expected mood strings.

Need help with the solution? https://www.unQbd.com/Solutions/CSharp7th/MakingDecisions

SWITCH

A **switch** statement is an alternative to an 'if' statement that is preferable when you have multiple discrete options to choose from. It's particularly useful when comparing a single variable to several possible constant values. While anything that can be done with a switch can also be done with 'if', switch statements can be clearer when dealing with many conditions.

In a switch statement, each option is a **case**, and a **default** case is used if none of the other cases match, similar to an 'else' statement in 'if' constructs. Unlike 'if' statements, case blocks in a switch don't require curly braces {} and are terminated with a **break;** to prevent fall-through.

Example: Switch

```
int optionPicked = 3;

switch (optionPicked)
{
case 1:
 Console.WriteLine("My number is 1");
 break;
case 2:
 Console.WriteLine("My number is 2");
 break;
case 3: // This case 3 is true.
 Console.WriteLine("My number is 3"); // Output: My number is 3
 break;
default:
 Console.WriteLine("Other option");
 break;
}
```

Cases without code will "fall through" until a break is encountered, allowing multiple cases to share the same code block. Note that C# 8.0 and later also support switch expressions, which can simplify some patterns further.

Example: Switch Case Fall Through

```csharp
int optionPicked = 2;

switch (optionPicked)
{
 case 1:
 case 2:
 case 3:
        Console.WriteLine("Low number selected"); // Output: Low number selected
        break;
 case 4:
 case 5:
 Console.WriteLine("Medium number selected");
 break;
 default:
 Console.WriteLine("Other number selected");
 break;
}
```

When dealing with strings in a switch statement, it's important to normalize the input to match the case expectations (e.g., using **.ToLower()** or **.ToUpper()** before the switch).

Full Example: String Switch

```csharp
Console.WriteLine("Type the name of a number: One, Two, or Three");

string num1 = Console.ReadLine().ToLower(); // If One was entered, it converts to one

switch (num1)
 {
  case "one":
  case "two":
        Console.WriteLine("Picked number 1 or 2");
        break;
  case "three":
        Console.WriteLine("Picked number 3");
        break;
  default:
        Console.WriteLine("Entered incorrect input");
        break;
 }
```

ACTIVITY: SWITCH

Activity: In this activity, you will create a console application that uses a switch statement to determine whether an entered letter is a vowel.

1. Display the prompt: "Enter a letter and find out if it is a vowel."

2. Capture the user's input and use a **switch** statement to check if the letter is a vowel and respond accordingly.

Expected Responses:

If a lowercase vowel is entered (a, e, i, o, u), the output will be:

```
The lowercase a is a vowel
```

If an uppercase vowel is entered (A, E, I, O, U), the output will be:

```
The uppercase A is a vowel
```

If any other letter or character is entered, the output will be:

```
The x is NOT a vowel
```

Hints:

- Implement a **switch** statement that evaluates the user's input. Remember to check for both uppercase and lowercase vowels.

- Use the **default** case in your **switch** statement to handle any input that is not a vowel.

Need help with the solution? https://www.unQbd.com/Solutions/CSharp7th/Switch

PARSE & TRYPARSE

Parse and **TryParse** are methods used to convert a string to another data type, such as an integer or a double. However, they differ significantly in how they handle invalid inputs.

When using Parse, ensure the string can be successfully converted to the target type. If the string is not a valid representation of the type, Parse will throw an exception, potentially causing the program to crash.

Example: Parse

```
int exampleOneInt = int.Parse("6"); // Safe as the string is a valid int.

string exampleTwo = "7";
int exampleTwoInt = int.Parse(exampleTwo); // Safe as exampleTwo is a valid int.

string exampleThree = "6.5";
double exampleThreeInt = double.Parse(exampleThree); // Parses to double.
```

TryParse is safer for handling potentially invalid input. It returns a Boolean indicating whether the conversion was successful, and sets the out parameter to the type's default value (0 for integers) if the conversion fails.

Example: TryParse

```
string example = "7";
int exampleInt;
int.TryParse(example, out exampleInt); // exampleInt is 7 if successful, 0 otherwise.
```

Optionally, the return value of TryParse can be saved to a Boolean variable to check if the conversion was successful.

Example: Saving Return Values of TryParse

```
string example = "9";
int resultInt;
bool isSuccess = int.TryParse(example, out resultInt); // isSuccess will be true if conversion is successful.
```

Example: Inline Out Variable with TryParse

```
string textExample = "10";
int.TryParse(textExample, out int textExampleInt); // Declartes textExampleInt inline.
```

Using the Inline Out variable in the approach above, it is not needed to declare the textExampleInt int beforehand.

Using TryParse within an if statement allows for immediate action based on the success of the conversion.

Example: TryParse with an 'If' Statement

```
string textExample = "8";
if (int.TryParse(textExample, out int textExampleInt))
{
        Console.WriteLine($"Conversion successful: {textExampleInt}");
}
else
{
        Console.WriteLine("Conversion failed. Default value of 0 assigned to textExampleInt.");
}
```

Example: Parse (Unsafe)

```
Console.WriteLine("Enter a number");
string text1 = Console.ReadLine();
int num1 = int.Parse(text1); // Unsafe: Can crash if input is invalid.

Console.WriteLine("Enter a second number");
int num2 = int.Parse(Console.ReadLine()); // Unsafe: Directly parsing user input.

Console.WriteLine($"The sum is {num1 + num2}");
```

Example: TryParse (Safe)

```
Console.WriteLine("Enter a number");
int.TryParse(Console.ReadLine(), out int num1);

Console.WriteLine("Enter a second number");
int.TryParse(Console.ReadLine(), out int num2);

Console.WriteLine($"The sum is {num1 + num2}");
```

TryParse is recommended when dealing with uncertain or user-provided data. It prevents exceptions and ensures that your program can handle invalid inputs gracefully.

ACTIVITY: TRYPARSE BILL CALCULATOR

Activity: This activity focuses on converting string inputs to numerical values and performing basic arithmetic operations. Create a Console Application for a bill calculator that follows these steps:

1. **Start with a Greeting**: Display the text "Bill Calculator".

2. **Gather User Input**: Ask the user three questions to input the cost of different items. Accept the user input for each question:

   A. "How much was the entrée?"

   B. "How much was the drink?"

   C. "How much was the dessert?"

3. **Calculate and Display the Total**: Convert the input values to a numerical data type suitable for arithmetic operations. Add all three values and display the total bill amount.

Expected Output Example:

```
Bill Calculator

How much was the entrée? 12.50

How much was the drink? 3.00

How much was the dessert? 5.75

The total bill is $21.25
```

Hints:

- Convert the string inputs to a numerical type, like double, using Double.Parse or Double.TryParse.

- Use string interpolation or concatenation to display the final bill amount.

Need help with the solution? https://www.unQbd.com/Solutions/CSharp7th/TryParse

LOOPS

Loops enable the repetition of a block of code multiple times. The four primary types of loops are **While**, **Do-While**, **For**, and **ForEach**.

While Loop: Executes as long as a specified condition is true.

Example: While Loop

```
int number = 0;

while (number < 10)
{
        Console.Write(number);
        number++; // Incrementing number by 1
}
 // Output: 0123456789
```

This loop outputs numbers from 0 to 9, incrementing *number* by 1 each iteration.

Do-While Loop: Executes the code block once before checking the condition, ensuring the block is executed at least once.

Example: Do-While Loop

```
int number = 0;

do
{
        Console.Write(number);
        number++;
}
while (number < 10);

// Output: 0123456789
```

For Loop: Commonly used when the number of iterations is known. It initializes the counter, checks the condition, and updates the counter in one line.

Example: For Loop

```
for (int i = 0; i < 10; i++)
{
        Console.Write(i); // Output: 0123456789
}
```

Note: Curly brackets are not necessary for single-line code in loops, but they are recommended for clarity.

ForEach Loop: Iterates over a collection, such as an array or list. (arrays and lists are covered in an upcoming sections).

Example: ForEach Loop

```
int[] numbers = new int[10] { 0, 1, 2, 3, 4, 5, 6, 7, 8, 9 };

foreach (int num in numbers)
{
        Console.Write(num); // Output: 0123456789
}
```

The next example demonstrates using both *While* and *For* loops to count up to a user-entered number.

Full Example: While and For Loops

```
Console.WriteLine("Enter a number to count up to it using a While loop");

int.TryParse(Console.ReadLine(), out int num1);
int counter = 0;

while (counter <= num1)
{
        Console.WriteLine(counter);
        counter++;
}

  Console.WriteLine("Enter a number to count up to it using a For loop");
  int.TryParse(Console.ReadLine(), out int num2);

for (int i = 0; i <= num2; i++)
{
        Console.WriteLine(i);
}
```

A **nested loop** occurs when one loop (the **child**) is placed inside another (the **parent**).

Example: Nested Loop

```
string playGame = "";
int counter = 0;

while (playGame != "Quit")
{
        while (counter < 5)
        {
                counter++;
                Console.WriteLine($"This number is from the nested loop: {counter}");
        }

        counter = 0;
        Console.WriteLine("Press Enter to display again or type Quit to exit.");
        playGame = Console.ReadLine();
}
```

Use **break** to exit a loop early.

Example: Break

```csharp
string computerNumber = "5";

while(true)
{
        Console.WriteLine("Guess what number I am thinking");
        string guessedNumber = Console.ReadLine();

        if (guessedNumber == computerNumber)
        {
                break;
        }
}
```

Use **continue** to skip the current iteration and proceeds to the next iteration of the loop.

Example: Continue

```csharp
for (int i = 0; i < 10; i++)
{
        if (i == 7)
        {
                continue; // Skip number 7
        }
        Console.WriteLine($"Number: {i}");
}
```

ACTIVITY: LOOPS COUNTER APP

Activity: This activity focuses on using loops to count up or down to a specific number. Create a Console Application for a Counter App that follows these steps:

1. **Start with a Greeting**: Display the text "Counter App".

2. **Gather User Input**: Ask the user two questions:

    A. "Enter in a number:"

    B. "Do you want to count Up or Down from that number? (Options: Up or Down):"

3. **Perform the Counting**: Based on the user's choice, count up or down to the entered number and display each step of the count.

Expected Output Example:

```
Counter App

Enter in a number: 3

Do you want to count Up or Down from that number? (Options: Up or Down): Up

Counting Up: 0

Counting Up: 1

Counting Up: 2

Counting Up: 3
```

Hints:

- Use a *for* loop for counting up or down based on the user's choice.

- Implement condition checking for the direction (Up or Down) using an *if* statement.

Need help with the solution? https://www.unQbd.com/Solutions/CSharp7th/Loops

ARRAYS

An **array** is a *collection* of elements of the same data type. Arrays can be used for storing, sorting, and iterating over a set of items.

Declaration: Use square brackets [] after the data type. It's common to use plural names for arrays for readability.

Example: Declare array

```
string[] foods;
```

Instantiation: Create an instance with the **new** keyword. The number inside the brackets indicates the array's size.

Example: Instantiate array

```
foods = new string[5];
```

Example: Combined Declaration and Instantiation

```
string[] foods = new string[5];
```

Assigning Values to Arrays: Arrays in C# are zero-indexed. The first element is at index 0.

Example: Direct Assignment

```
foods[0] = "Pizza";
```

Example: Initialization with Values

```
string[] drinks = new string[5] { "Pepsi", "Sprite", "", "", "" };
```

Example: Accessing Array Elements

```
string[] animals = { "Cat", "Dog" };
Console.WriteLine(animals[0]); // Output: Cat
```

Iterating Over Arrays: Using a *foreach* loop is a common way to iterate over all elements.

Example: Display All Items of an Array

```
string[] foods = { "Pizza", "Burger" };

foreach (string food in foods)
{
        Console.WriteLine($"The food item is {food}.");
}
```

Example: Array Sorting and Length

```
Array.Sort(someNumbers);
```

Full Example: Sort and array length. The **length** property in this example is used to determine how many loops should occur.

```
int[] someNumbers = { 21, 22, 50, 3, 6 };

Array.Sort(someNumbers);

for (int i = 0; i < someNumbers.Length; i++)
{
        Console.Write($"{ someNumbers[i]} "); // Output: 3 6 21 22 50
}
```

The above example uses "Array.Sort()". Sort is a method within the Array class that organizes the contents of an array numerically and alphabetically. The Array class has other methods as well, such as "Array.Reverse()".

ACTIVITY: ARRAYS MONTHS APP

Activity: Create a Console Application that allows a user to input a number (1-12) to display the corresponding month name or type "Display All" to show all months.

1. **Initial Prompt**:

    - Display: "Enter a month (1-12) to display the month name or type Display All".

2. **Display Specific Month**:

    - If a user enters a number between 1 and 12, display the corresponding month.

    - Example: If input is 2, output should be February.

3. **Display All Months**:

    - If the user types "Display All", output all the months in order.

4. **Handle Invalid Input**:

    - If an incorrect input (like **15** or a non-numeric value) is entered, display: "Not a valid input".

Expected Output: If a user enters '2'

February

Expected Output: If a user enters 'Display All'

January
February
March ... continues on until December

Expected Output: If a user enters '15'

Not a valid input

Need help with the solution? https://www.unQbd.com/Solutions/CSharp7th/Arrays

ARRAYS: 2-D AND 3-D

In the previous section, we discussed **one-dimensional (1-D) arrays**. Here, we'll explore **two-dimensional (2-D)** and **three-dimensional (3-D) arrays**, which are useful for more complex data structures.

Two-Dimensional (2-D) Arrays:

2-D arrays require two indices, representing rows and columns. Use a comma inside square brackets to declare a 2-D array.

Example: Declare a 2-D Array

```
string[,] myGameMap = new string[,]
{
        // Empty 2D array, dimensions to defined later
};
```

Full Example: 2-D Array

```
// 2-D Array for a game map
string[,] myGameMap = new string[,]
{
        {"Scary Room1", "Safe Room2", "Safe Room3"},        // Row 0
        {"Dangerous Room4", "Safe Room5", "Safe Room6"}, // Row 1
        {"Safe Room7", "Scary Room8", "Safe Room9"}        // Row 2
};

// Accessing elements: [row, column]
Console.WriteLine(myGameMap[0, 0]); // Output: Scary Room1
Console.WriteLine(myGameMap[1, 0]); // Output: Dangerous Room4
Console.WriteLine(myGameMap[2, 2]); // Output: Safe Room9
```

Three-Dimensional (3-D) Arrays:

3-D arrays add a third dimension, often conceptualized as depth, to the data structure. Use two commas in the square brackets for declaring a 3-D array.

Example: Declare a 3-D Array

```
string[,,] arrayExample3D = new string[,,]
{
        // Empty 3D array, dimensions to be defined later
};
```

Full Example: 3-D Array

```
string[,,] arrayExample3D = new string[,,]
 {

   {{"Mariah ", "created "}, {"a 3-D ", "array example."}}, // Row 0, Columns 0 & 1, Depths 0 & 1
   {{"They can ", "become "}, {"complex ", "very quickly."}}, // Row 1, Columns 0 & 1, Depths 0 &
   {{"Hoping ", "these "}, {"colors will ", "help!"}}, // Row 2, Columns 0 & 1, Depths 0 &
 };

        // Accessing elements: [Row, Column, Depth]
Console.Write(); // Output: Mariah
Console.Write(arrayExample3D[0, 0, 1]); // Output: created
Console.Write(arrayExample3D[0, 1, 0]); // Output: a 3-D
Console.Write(arrayExample3D[0, 1, 1]); // Output: array example.
Console.WriteLine();
Console.Write(arrayExample3D[1, 0, 0]); // Output: They can
Console.Write(arrayExample3D[1, 0, 1]); // Output: become
Console.Write(arrayExample3D[1, 1, 0]); // Output: complex
Console.Write(arrayExample3D[1, 1, 1]); // Output: very quickly

// Output:
// Mariah created a 3-D array example.
// The can become complex very quickly
```

Note: Understanding and visualizing 3-D arrays can be challenging, especially for beginners. It helps to think of a 3-D array as a collection of 2-D arrays stacked on top of each other, each 2-D array representing a different "depth" level.

ACTIVITY: 2-D ARRAYS HOTEL APP

Activity: This activity uses a two-dimensional array to manage and check the occupancy of hotel rooms. Create a Console Application to check the occupancy of rooms in a hotel.

1. **Initial Display:**

   - Display a message: "Which floor do you want to check for occupancy? (0 or 1)".

2. **Floor Selection:**

   - Prompt the user to enter a floor number (0 or 1).

   - Save the user's response to a variable.

3. **Room Selection:**

   - Display a message: "Which room do you want to check for occupancy? (0, 1, or 2)".

   - Prompt the user to enter a room number (0, 1, or 2).

   - Save the user's response to another variable.

4. **Occupancy Check:**

   - Use the floor and room numbers to check the occupancy from a 2-D array.

   - Display the floor, room number, and occupancy status (e.g., who is in the room or if it is empty).

Example Outputs:

- If the user inputs floor 0, room 1, and the room is occupied by "John Doe", display: "Floor 0, Room 1 is occupied by John Doe."

- If the user inputs floor 1, room 2, and the room is empty, display: "Floor 1, Room 2 is Empty."

Need help with the solution? https://www.unQbd.com/Solutions/CSharp7th/TwoDArrays

ARRAYS: JAGGED

A **jagged array** is a unique array structure in which each element of the main array can be an array itself, and these inner arrays can have different lengths. This flexibility allows for a more complex and variable data structure compared to regular multi-dimensional arrays.

Example: Declare a Jagged Array

```
string[][] jaggedEx = new string[3][]; // An array with 3 array elements
```

Example: Assign Arrays to a Jagged Array

```
jaggedEx[0] = new string[2]; // First element is an array with 2 strings
jaggedEx[1] = new string[5]; // Second element is an array with 5 strings
jaggedEx[2] = new string[8]; // Third element is an array with 8 strings
```

Here, *jaggedEx* is a jagged array containing three arrays of different sizes.

Example: Declare and Initialize a Jagged Array

```
string[][] jaggedEx = new string[3][]
{
        new string[2], // First element with 2 strings
        new string[5], // Second element with 5 strings
        new string[8], // Third element with 8 strings
};
```

Example: Assign Values to Elements in a Jagged Array

```
jaggedEx[1][4] = "Store this string in Array 1, Element 4";
```

Here, we are assigning a value to the fifth element (index 4) of the second array (index 1) in the jagged array.

Full Example: Jagged Array

```csharp
string[][] classStudents = new string[2][]
{
        new string[2], // Classroom students
        new string[1] // Online students
};

classStudents[0][0] = "Sergio";     // In-classroom student
classStudents[0][1] = "Jonathan"; // In-classroom student
classStudents[1][0] = "Aria";       // Online student

Console.WriteLine($"{classStudents[0][0]} and {classStudents[0][1]}: Classroom students");
// Output: Sergio and Jonathan: Classroom students

Console.WriteLine($"{classStudents[1][0]}: Online student");
// Output: Aria: Online student
```

In this example, *classStudents* is a jagged array representing two types of students: those in the classroom and those online. It showcases how jagged arrays can be used to store and organize data of varying lengths effectively.

METHODS

A **method** is a block of code designed to perform a specific task. It enhances code reusability and clarity. To utilize a method, you first define it and then **call** (or invoke) it as needed. Methods can be invoked numerous times.

A method's full syntax comprises several parts:

```csharp
public static int AddTwoNumbers(int num1, int num2)
{
        return num1 + num2;
}
```

- **Access Modifier:** Determines the visibility of the method. Common modifiers include **public**, **private**, **protected**, and **internal**. The default is private.

- **Static Modifier:** Indicates that the method belongs to the class itself rather than an instance of the class. Omitting **static** implies an instance method.

- **Return Type:** Specifies the type of value the method returns. Use **void** if the method does not return a value.

- **Method Name:** Should be descriptive and follow C# naming conventions.

- **Parameters:** Define the data passed to the method. Parameters are optional, and methods can have none.

Example: Method Returning No Value

```csharp
static void DisplayWelcomeMessage()
{
        Console.WriteLine("Welcome, Guest");
}

DisplayWelcomeMessage (); // Call the method
```

Methods can also have **parameters**. Parameters pass values from **arguments** into methods. The parameter refers to the *name* and the arguments are the *values* sent to the method. The example below notes where each is located.

Example: Method with Parameters and Return Type

```
static void GreetUser (string name) // Parameter is "name"
{
        Console.WriteLine($"Welcome, {name}");    // Output: Welcome, Adam
}

GreetUser ("Adam");  // Call the method and pass the argument "Adam"
```

Parameters can be optional by giving them a default value. In the example below, following the parameter "name", the default value "Guest" is assigned to the parameter, making it optional.

Example: Method with an Optional Parameter

```
static void GreetUser(string name = "Guest")
{
        Console.WriteLine($"Hello, {name}");
}

GreetUser();         // Output: Hello, Guest
GreetUser("Adam"); // Output: Hello, Adam
```

Example: Method that *Returns a Value* and *Accepts a Parameter*

```
static int AddThreeNumbers(int num1, int num2, int num3)
{
        return = num1 + num2 + num3;
}

int a = 5, b = 2;
int combinedValue = AddThreeNumbers(a, b, 8);
Console.WriteLine($"{a} + {b} + 8 = {combinedValue}");  // Output: 5 + 2 + 8 = 15
```

Full Example: Passing an *Object* to a Method (objects and classes covered in the upcoming "Classes" section)

```
Player player1 = new() { Name = "ABC", Health = 100 };

Combat.FightBattle(player1);
Console.WriteLine($"{player1.Name} has {player1.Health} health"); // Output: ABC has 80 health

public class Player
{
        public string Name { get; set; }
        public int Health { get; set; } = 100;
}

public static class Combat
{
        public static void FightBattle(Player thePlayer)
        {
                thePlayer.Health = thePlayer.Health - 20; // Decrease health by 20
        }
}
```

Arguments can be passed by *reference*, not by value. Pass references with the **ref** keyword; changes made in a method for a reference will affect the original value outside the method.

Example: Passing Arguments by Reference

```
static void PlayerDamaged(ref int playerHealth)
{
        playerHealth -= 20;
}

int playerHealth = 100;
PlayerDamaged(ref playerHealth);
Console.WriteLine(playerHealth);  // Output: 80
```

Best Practices:

- Keep methods focused on a single task for clarity and maintainability.

- Strive for readability in method names and code structure.

Remember, a well-written method not only performs its intended task efficiently but is also easy to understand and maintain.

ACTIVITY: METHODS

Activity: This activity focuses on creating a method to determine if a number is positive or negative, or neither. Create a Console Application named PositiveOrNegativeApp that meets the following requirements:

1. **Initial Setup:**

   - Display the message: "Positive or Negative?".

   - Prompt the user with: "Enter a number:".

2. **Method Creation:**

   - Create a method named DeterminePositiveOrNegative that takes an integer as a parameter and returns a string indicating whether the number is positive, negative, or neither.

Expected Output: If a user enters '5'

```
Positive or Negative?

Enter a number: 5

5 is positive.
```

Expected Output: If a user enters '0'

```
Positive or Negative?

Enter a number: 0

0 is neither positive nor negative.
```

Hints:

   - Use int.TryParse for converting user input to an integer and handling non-numeric input.

Need help with the solution? https://www.unQbd.com/Solutions/CSharp7th/Methods

CLASSES

A **class** is a blueprint or template for creating **objects**. It groups related methods and variables with common attributes. A single class can be used to **instantiate** multiple objects.

Example: Create a Class

```
class Card
{
        // Properties with get-set accessors (covered in an upcoming section)
        public string Name { get; set; }
        public int Value { get; set; }
        public string Suit { get; set; } = "Heart"; // Default value of "Heart"
}
```

Example: Instantiate an Object

```
Card Card1 = new();
```

Example: Assign Values to an Object

```
Card1.Name = "King";
Card1.Value = 13;
```

Example: Instantiate an Object and Assign Values

```
Card Card2 = new()
{
        Name = "Nine",
        Value = 9,
        Suit = "Spade"
};
```

Example: Display Output from an Object

```
Console.WriteLine($"Card1 Suit: {Card1.Suit} Name: {Card1.Name} Value: {Card1.Value}");
Console.WriteLine($"Card2 Suit: {Card2.Suit} Name: {Card2.Name} Value: {Card2.Value}");
```

Full Example: Class with a Method

```csharp
class Card
{
        public string Name { get; set; }
        public int Value { get; set; }
        public string Suit { get; set; } = "Heart"; // Set a default value of "Heart"

        public void DisplayCard()
        {
                Console.WriteLine($"Card Suit: {Suit} Name: {Name} Value: {Value}");
        }
}

// Instantiate objects and call a method
Card Card1 = new() { Name = "King", Value = 13 };
Card Card2 = new() { Name = "Nine", Value = 9, Suit = "Spade" };

Card1.DisplayCard(); // Output: Card Suit: Heart Name: King Value: 13
Card2.DisplayCard(); // Output: Card Suit: Spade Name: Nine Value: 9
```

In the Card class, the DisplayCard() method is an instance method, which means it's called on instances of the class (e.g., Card1 and Card2), not on the class itself.

Example: Using an Array with Class

```csharp
Card[] DeckOfCards = new Card[]
{
        new Card {Name = "Ace", Value = 1, Suit = "Heart"},
        new Card {Name = "Two", Value = 2, Suit = "Heart"},
        new Card {Name = "Three", Value = 3, Suit = "Heart"}
        // Continue adding cards...
};
```

Here, DeckOfCards is an array of Card objects, demonstrating how a class can be used as a type in collections.

ACTIVITY: CLASSES – HOUSE INVENTORY APP

Activity: Create a Console Application for a House Inventory App that meets the following requirements:

1. **Initial Message**: Display "Press Enter to see all available house inventory". Ensure the program waits for the user to press Enter before proceeding.

2. **House Class**: Create a **House** class with the following properties:

   - **Address** (string)

   - **Size** (integer or double, representing square footage)

   - **Price** (decimal, representing the cost of the house)

3. **House Array**: Create an array to store at least three fictional houses. Initialize this array with sample data.

4. **Display Method**: Create a method within your program that displays all the houses from the array.

Example Output:

```
Press Enter to see all available house inventory

House 1: Address: 123 Maple Street / Size: 2000 sq ft / Price: $350,000

House 2: Address: 456 Oak Avenue / Size: 1500 sq ft / Price: $275,000

House 3: Address: 789 Pine Road / Size: 1800 sq ft / Price: $300,000
```

Need help with the solution? https://www.unQbd.com/Solutions/CSharp7th/Classes

GET-SET PROPERTIES

Get-Set properties are a way to control access to class data, promoting encapsulation in object-oriented programming. They combine aspects of both fields and methods, allowing controlled access (read and/or write) to private class fields. Encapsulation enhances data integrity and provides a clear interface for class interactions.

Example: Full Declaration of a Property

```csharp
private string _myProperty;  // Private field
public string MyProperty    // Public property
{
        get { return _myProperty; } // Get method
        set { _myProperty = value; } // Set method
}
```

In this example, MyProperty provides controlled access to the private field _myProperty.

Full Example: Get-Set Property with Logic

```csharp
public class Month
{
  private int _theMonth;
  public int TheMonthVerify
  {
        get
        {
                if ((_theMonth > 12) || (_theMonth < 1))
                {
                        _theMonth = 0;
                }
                return _theMonth;
        }
        set { _theMonth = value; }
  }
}
```

This example includes logic within the get accessor to validate the month value.

For cases requiring no additional logic, **auto-implemented properties** simplify property declaration. The compiler automatically creates and manages the private field.

Example: Auto-Implemented Properties

```csharp
public string MyProperty { get; set; } // Auto-implemented
public int MyNumber { get; set; } = 5; // With default value
```

Example: Read-Only and Private Set Properties

```csharp
public string MyProperty { get; } // Read-only property

public class Vehicle
{
        public Vehicle(int id)
        {
                CarID = id;
        }

  public int CarID { get; private set; } // Private set accessor
}
```

Object initializer syntax allows setting multiple properties during object creation, making the code more readable and concise.

Full Example: Object Initializer Syntax

```csharp
public class Vehicle
{
        public string Brand { get; set; }
        public string Color { get; set; }
}

Vehicle car1 = new() { Brand = "Toyota", Color = "Red" };
Vehicle car2 = new();
car2.Brand = "Ford";
car2.Color = "White";
```

CLASSES: STATIC

The **static** keyword denotes that the class is singular and cannot be instantiated. In other words, you cannot create an instance (object) of a static class. Furthermore, all members of a static class, including methods and fields, must be static. Static classes are also sealed, which means they cannot be inherited.

Example: Static Class

```
static class OnlyOneHouse
{
        public static string Color { get; set; } = "Red";
}
```

Full Example: Static Class with Properties and Method

```
static class OnlyOneHouse
{
        // Static properties for the House class
        public static int Height { get; set; } = 10;  // Initial value
        public static int Width { get; } = 5; // Read-only property with initial value
        public static int Size { get; private set; } // Private setter to control access
        public static string Color { get; set; } = "Red";

        static OnlyOneHouse()
        {
                Size = Height * Width;
        }

        public static void DisplayHouse()
        {
                Console.WriteLine($"Size of House: {Size} and color {Color}");
        }
}

// Using the static class
OnlyOneHouse.DisplayHouse(); // Output: Size of House: 50 and color Red
```

In this example, OnlyOneHouse is a static class with static properties Height, Width, Size, and Color. The static constructor initializes Size based on the values of Height and Width. The DisplayHouse method outputs the details of the house.

CLASSES: CONSTRUCTOR

A **constructor** is a special method in a class that executes when an instance of the class is created. Constructors have the same name as the class and can be overloaded to provide different ways of initializing objects. They do not have a return type. While they are typically instance methods, C# also supports static constructors for initializing static members or performing certain actions once at the class level.

Example: Parameterless Constructor

```csharp
public class Person
{
        public Person()
        {
                // This is a parameterless constructor that initializes the object without any arguments
        }
}
```

Full Example: Overloaded Constructors

```csharp
public class Person
{
        // The 'Name' property is publicly accessible but can only be set within the class
        public string Name { get; private set; }

        // Parameterless constructor
        public Person()
        {
                Name = "Unnamed";
        }

        // Constructor with one parameter
        public Person(string name)
        {
                Name = name;
        }
}
// Using the constructors
Person person1 = new Person(); // Calls parameterless constructor
Console.WriteLine(person1.Name); // Output: Unnamed

Person person2 = new Person("Adam"); // Calls constructor with one argument
Console.WriteLine(person2.Name); // Output: Adam
```

With C# 13, **primary constructors** for non-record classes and structs have been introduced. This feature allows parameters to be added directly to the class or struct declaration, streamlining the initialization of objects.

Example: Primary Constructor

```csharp
public class Person(string firstName, string lastName)
{
        public string Name => $"{firstName {lastName}";
}
```

Primary constructors allow you to define constructor parameters directly in the class definition, reducing boilerplate code and making it more readable. This feature is particularly useful for classes with straightforward initialization needs.

MINI QUIZ: CLASS CONSTRUCTOR

Mini Quiz

1. Can a static class in C# have an instance constructor?

    A. True
    B. False

2. Can a constructor in C# have a return value?

    A. True
    B. False

3. Does a constructor in C# have to have the exact same name as its class?

    A. True
    B. False

4. Can constructors in C# be overloaded?

    A. True
    B. False

Mini Quiz Answers

4. A
3. A
2. B
1. B

CLASSES: INHERITANCE

Classes can **inherit** from other classes, allowing a **derived** (child) class to acquire all features of a **base** (parent) class. This mechanism facilitates code reuse and polymorphism. However, C# supports single inheritance, meaning a class can inherit from only one other class at a time.

Example: Inheritance

```csharp
// TheFirstClass is the base class
public class TheFirstClass
{
        // Base class properties and methods
}

// TheSecondClass inherits all features of TheFirstClass
public class TheSecondClass : TheFirstClass
{
        // Inherits all features of TheFirstClass
}
```

Full Example: Inheriting Properties

```csharp
public class CarBaseClass
{
        public string Brand { get; set; }
        public int Wheels { get; } = 4;
}

public class CarSedanDerivedClass : CarBaseClass
{
        public int Doors { get; } = 2;
}

// Creating and using an object of the derived class
CarSedanDerivedClass car1 = new();
car1.Brand = "Tesla";
Console.WriteLine($"A {car1.Brand} has {car1.Wheels} wheels and {car1.Doors} doors");
// Output: A Tesla has 4 wheels and 2 doors
```

C# allows for **transient** inheritance, enabling a class hierarchy where a class can inherit from another class, which itself is a derived class.

Full Example: Transient Inheritance

```csharp
// Base class
public class BaseClassExample
{
        public int TheBaseProperty { get; } = 5;
}

// Intermediate derived class
public class AClassExample : BaseClassExample
{
        // Inherits TheBaseProperty
}

// Further derived class
public class BClassExample : AClassExample
{
        // Inherits TheBaseProperty from BaseClassExample indirectly
}

BClassExample obj1 = new();
Console.WriteLine(obj1.TheBaseProperty); // Output: 5
```

A **sealed** class cannot be inherited. Use sealed classes to prevent further inheritance, which can be useful for security, to avoid unintended usage, or in certain cases to enhance performance.

```csharp
// This class cannot be inherited
sealed class ExampleSealedClass
{
        // Class implementation
}
```

MINI QUIZ: CLASS INHERITANCE

Mini Quiz

1. Does C# allows for multiple inheritance?

    A. True

    B. False

2. Is the following code valid in C#?

```csharp
public class SecondClass : BaseClass, FirstClass
{
        // Empty class
}
```

    A. True

    B. False

3. Is the following code valid in C#?

```csharp
public class BaseClass
{
        // Empty class
}

public class FirstClass : BaseClass
{
        // Empty class
}

public class SecondClass : FirstClass
{
        // Empty class
}
```

    A. True

    B. False

Mini Quiz Answers

3. A

2. B

1. B

METHODS: OVERLOAD

Method overloading allows multiple methods to have the same name but different signatures. A method's signature includes the number and types of its parameters. The order of parameters can also play a role in differentiating overloaded methods. The C# compiler selects the appropriate overloaded method based on the arguments passed during the method call, ensuring that the best match is used.

Example: Method Overloading

```csharp
class ExampleOverloadMethod
{
        public static void DisplayMe()
        {
                Console.WriteLine("Result: Nothing to Display");
        }

        public static void DisplayMe(string theString)
        {
                Console.WriteLine($"The string {theString} was called");
        }

        public static void DisplayMe(int theInt)
        {
                Console.WriteLine($"The int {theInt} was called");
        }

        public static void DisplayMe(int theInt1, int theInt2)
        {
                Console.WriteLine($"The total of the 2 numbers is {theInt1 + theInt2}");
        }
}
```

In this example, *DisplayMe* is overloaded four times, each with a different signature.

Example: Using Overloaded Methods

```csharp
ExampleOverloadMethod.DisplayMe();                    // Output: "Result: Nothing to Display"
ExampleOverloadMethod.DisplayMe("Hello World"); // Output: "The string Hello World was called"
ExampleOverloadMethod.DisplayMe(215);                 // Output: "The int 215 was called"
ExampleOverloadMethod.DisplayMe(215, 500);            // Output: "The total of those 2 numbers is 715"
```

The compiler determines which *DisplayMe* method to invoke based on the provided arguments.

MINI QUIZ: METHOD OVERLOADING

Mini Quiz

1. Is the following a valid method overload?

```csharp
class QuizDisplayMe
{
        public static void DisplayMe(string theString)
        {
                // ... method body
        }

        public static void DisplayMe(string anotherString)
        {
                // ... method body
        }
}
```

    A. True

    B. False

2. Is the following a valid method overload?

```csharp
class QuizDisplayMe
{
        public static void DisplayMe(string theString)
        {
                // ... method body
        }

        public static void DisplayMe(int theInt)
        {
                // ... method body
        }
}
```

    A. True

    B. False

Mini Quiz Answers

1. B – The methods have the same name and parameter types, differing only in parameter names. This does not constituted a valid overload in C#.

2. A

METHODS: RECURSION

Recursion is a programming technique where a method calls itself to solve a problem. A method that uses this technique is known as a **recursive method**.

Example: Recursive Method

```
public static double RecursiveMethod()
{
        // Warning: This method will cause a stack overflow because it has no termination condition
        return RecursiveMethod();
}
// Note: The above call is unsafe and will cause a runtime error if executed
// double result = RecursiveMethod();
```

Full Example: Recursive Method for Input Validation

```
class InputValidator
{
        public static string VerifyWord()
        {
                Console.WriteLine("Choose: Up, Down");
                string direction = Console.ReadLine();

                if (direction == "Up" || direction == "Down")
                {
                        return direction;
                }
                return VerifyWord(); // Recursive call for invalid input
        }
}

string directionToGo = InputValidator.VerifyWord();
Console.WriteLine($"You chose: {directionToGo}");
```

Full Example: Recursive Method for Calculating Factorials (Advanced)

```csharp
class FactorialCalculator
{
        // A factorial is the multiplication of every number below it.
        // For example: The factorial of 4 equals (1 * 2 * 3 * 4 = 24)
        public static int Factorial(int number)
        {
                if (number == 0)
                {
                        return 1; // Base case for termination
                }
                return number * Factorial(number - 1); // Recursive call
        }
}
int numberEntered = 4;
int factorial = FactorialCalculator.Factorial(numberEntered);
Console.WriteLine($"Factorial of {numberEntered} = {factorial}");
```

Indirect recursion occurs when a method invokes another method, and this sequence of calls eventually leads back to the original method.

Full Example: Indirect Recursion

```csharp
class OddEvenChecker
{
        public static bool IsOdd(int number)
        {
                if (number == 0)
                {
                        return false;
                }
                return IsEven(Math.Abs(number) - 1);
        }
        public static bool IsEven(int number)
        {
                if (number == 0)
                {
                        return true;
                }
                return IsOdd(Math.Abs(number) - 1);
        }
}
int number = 7;
bool isOdd = OddEvenChecker.IsOdd(number);
Console.WriteLine($"Is the number {number} odd? {isOdd}");
```

METHODS: NAMED ARGUMENTS

Named arguments improve the clarity of method calls by specifying which parameter each argument corresponds to. This is especially useful in methods with multiple parameters, where it can be challenging to track which argument is which.

Example: Calling a Method with a Named Argument

```
AMethodName(Person: "Matt"); // It's clear that "Matt" is for the Person parameter
```

Full Example: Named Arguments

```
// Without named arguments, it's unclear what the numbers represent
CharacterDescription("Bob", 42, 72, 61);

// With one named argument, it's clearer that 61 is the level
CharacterDescription("Bob", 42, 72, level: 61);

// With three named arguments, each value is clearly associated with a parameter
CharacterDescription("Bob", age: 42, height: 72, level: 61);

// With all named arguments, the method call is very clear
CharacterDescription(name: "Bob", age: 42, height: 72, level: 61);

// TIP: Method arguments can be entered on multiple lines for additional clarity
CharacterDescription(name: "Bob",
                     age: 42,
                     height: 72,
                     level: 61);

static void CharacterDescription(string name, int age, int height, int level)
{
        Console.WriteLine($"{name}: level {level}, {age} years old, and height of {height} inches.");
}
```

In the above examples, using named arguments helps to clarify what each parameter in the *CharacterDescription* method represents. This is particularly helpful when a method has multiple parameters, and it can be challenging to remember the order and meaning of each.

METHOD: VIRTUAL

Virtual methods allow derived classes to override methods defined in a base class. This is done using the *virtual* keyword in the base class and the *override* keyword in the derived class. Virtual methods enable polymorphic behavior, where a method can have different implementations in different classes.

Example: Virtual Method

```
public virtual void Sound()
{
        Console.WriteLine("Generic Noise");
}
```

Full Example: Virtual Method

```
// Base class
class Animal
{
        public virtual void Sound()
        {
                Console.WriteLine("Generic Noise");
        }
}

// Derived class
class Dog : Animal
{
        public override void Sound()
        {
                Console.WriteLine("Bark");
        }
}

Animal anyAnimal = new();
anyAnimal.Sound(); // Output: Generic Noise

Dog aDog = new();
aDog.Sound(); // Output: Bark
```

In the above example, when *Sound()* is called on an instance of *Animal*, it outputs "Generic Noise". However, when the same method is called on an instance of *Dog*, it outputs "Bark". This is because the *Dog* class overrides the *Sound* method with its own implementation.

CLASSES: ABSTRACT

Abstract classes are used as a base for other classes. They cannot be instantiated directly and are intended to outline methods and properties that are common to all subclasses. Any **abstract methods** defined in an abstract class must be implemented by the derived classes, while virtual methods provide a default implementation that can optionally be overridden.

Example: Abstract Class

```
public abstract class Talk
{
        // An empty abstract class
}
```

Full Example: Abstract Class

```
// Abstract class with abstract and virtual methods
public abstract class Talk
{
        // Abstract method must be implemented in derived class
        public abstract void Greeting();

        // Virtual method provides a default implementation but can be optionally overridden
        public virtual void Goodbye()
        {
                Console.WriteLine("Goodbye!");
        }
}

// Derived class implementing abstract method
public class SpanishLanguage : Talk
{
        public override void Greeting()
        {
                Console.WriteLine("Hola");
        }
}

SpanishLanguage languageSelected = new();
languageSelected.Greeting(); // Output: Hola
languageSelected.Goodbye(); // Output: Goodbye!
```

In the above example, *SpanishLanguage* is a derived class of *Talk*. It is required to implement the abstract *Greeting* method, while it inherits the *Goodbye* method without overriding it. The result is that calling *Greeting* on a *SpanishLanguage* object outputs "Hola", and calling *Goodbye* outputs "Goodbye!".

Partial classes allow a class to be split across multiple files. This feature is useful for separating complex classes into manageable parts, for working in large teams, or when dealing with auto-generated code like GUIs in Visual Studio. The *partial* keyword indicates that the class, struct, or interface is defined across multiple files within the same namespace.

Example: Partial Class

```csharp
public partial class PartialExample
{
        // Part of a partial class
}
```

Full Example: Partial Class

```csharp
Employee employee1 = new();
employee1.Name = "John";
employee1.WelcomeMessage(employee1.Name); // Output: John, welcome to our company

// First part of the partial class definition
public partial class Employee
{
        public string Name { get; set; }
}
// Second part of the partial class definition
public partial class Employee
{
        public void WelcomeMessage(string name)
        {
                Console.WriteLine($"{name}, welcome to our company");
        }
}
```

Partial classes are particularly useful in scenarios involving auto-generated code, like in GUI development with Visual Studio, where part of the class is generated by a designer tool. While partial classes can help organize large classes, it's often better to refactor large classes into smaller, more focused classes. However, when a class's functionality spans multiple concerns that are logically related but physically separate (like design code versus business logic), partial classes can be a sensible solution.

ACCESS MODIFIER: PUBLIC, INTERNAL, PROTECTED, AND PRIVATE

Access modifiers control the visibility of classes and members (methods, properties, etc.) to other parts of a program.

- **Public:** Accessible from any other code in the same assembly or another assembly that references it. Used when you want the member to be accessible everywhere.

- **Internal:** Accessible only within its own assembly. It's the default for classes if no access modifier is specified. Useful for internal workings of an assembly that aren't exposed externally.

- **Protected:** Accessible only within its own class and by derived class instances. Used when you want to allow access to derived classes but not to the outside world.

- **Private:** Accessible only within the defining class. It's the default for class members if no access modifier is specified. Used to hide the member from other parts of the program.

- **Protected Internal:** Accessible within its own assembly or by derived class instances. Combines the functionalities of both protected and internal.

- **Private Protected:** Accessible within its containing class or types derived from the containing class in the same assembly. It is a stricter version of protected internal.

Full Example: Public, Internal, Protected, and Private

```
internal class VehicleOption
{
        public int a = 1;      // Public: Accessible from anywhere
        protected int b = 2;  // Protected: Accessible in this class and derived classes
        private int c = 3;     // Private: Accessible only in this class
}

class AdvancedOption: VehicleOption
{
        public AdvancedOption()
        {
                a = 7; // Accessible because 'a' is public
                b = 8; // Accessible because 'b' is protected and AdvancedOption is a derived class
                // c = 9; // Error: 'c' is private and only accessible within VehicleOption
        }
{

VehicleOption car = new();
car.a = 4; // Accessible as 'a' is public
// car.b = 5; // Error: 'b' is protected and only accessible within VehicleOption or its derived classes
// car.c = 6; // Error: 'c' is private and only accessible within VehicleOption
```

In this example, *VehicleOption* has three fields with different access levels. The *AdvancedOption* class, which inherits from *VehicleOption*, demonstrates how these access levels control visibility. Understanding these modifiers is crucial for encapsulating and protecting the data and behavior of your classes.

MINI QUIZ: ACCESS MODIFIERS

Mini Quiz

1. Which of the following gives the most access?

    A. Internal
    B. Private
    C. Public
    D. Protected

2. What is the default modifier for a method?

    A. Internal
    B. Private
    C. Public
    D. Protected

3. What is the default modifier for a class?

    A. Internal
    B. Private
    C. Public
    D. Protected

4. Which of the following gives the least access?

    A. Internal
    B. Private
    C. Public
    D. Protected

Mini Quiz Answers

4. B
3. A
2. B
1. C

RANDOM NUMBER

Creating random numbers is a common requirement in software applications. The **Random** class provides various methods to generate random numbers.

Example: Random Number from *0 to 2,147,483,646*

```
Random random = new(); // Instantiate an object of the Random class

// The Next() method returns a non-negative random integer.
int randomNumber = random.Next(); // This will generate a number between 0 and Int32.MaxValue.
```

Example: Specifying Maximum Value in Next Method

```
Random random = new(); // Instantiate an object of the Random class

// Generate a non-negative random integer less than the specified maximum.
int randomNumber = random.Next(11);  // This will generate a number from 0 to 10.
```

Example: Specifying Range with Min and Max Values in Next Method

```
Random random = new(); // Instantiate an object of the Random class

// Generate a random integer within a specified range.
int randomNumber = random.Next(10, 21); // This will generate a number from 10 to 20.
```

Full Example: Random Number in a Method

```
Console.WriteLine(RandomNumberMethod(5001));  // Output will vary from 1 to 5000.

static int RandomNumberMethod(int maxExclusive)
{
        Random random = new(); // Instantiate an object of the Random class
        return random.Next(1, maxExclusive); // Generates a number between 1 and maxExclusive.
}
```

If multiple random numbers are needed in rapid succession, it's more efficient to reuse the same Random instance rather than creating new ones each time.

ACTIVITY: RANDOM NUMBER GUESSING GAME

Activity: Create a Console Application for a Guessing Game that allows a user to guess a computer-generated random number.

1. **Initial Prompt:** Display the message: "Guess the computer's number between 1 and 10. You have 3 attempts!".

2. **Random Number Generation:** Have the computer generate a random number between 1 and 10.

3. **Guessing Mechanism:** Allow the user to input guesses and limit the number of attempts to 3.

4. **Feedback Mechanism:** After each guess, inform the user if their guess was too low, too high, or correct.

5. **End of Game:** After the user guesses correctly or exhausts all attempts, reveal the correct number and end the game.

Example Output:

```
Guess the computer's number between 1 and 10. You have 3 attempts!

Enter your guess: 5

Too high! Try again.

Enter your guess: 3

Too low! Try again.

Enter your guess: 4

Correct! Well done.
```

Hints:

- Consider using *int.TryParse* for input validation to ensure the user inputs a number.

- Consider using a *for* or *while* loop for allowing up to three guesses.

Need help with the solution? https://www.unQbd.com/Solutions/CSharp7th/RandomNumber

MEMORY: HEAP AND STACK

When a variable is declared, it is allocated in **RAM**. This allocation includes the value for value types or a reference (address) for reference types, but not the variable's name.

Variables are categorized into two main types: **value types** and **reference types**. Value types, like *int* and *bool*, are stored on the **stack**. This area is used for static memory allocation, which includes local variables and keeps track of the program's state.

On the other hand, reference types, such as strings, arrays, and objects, are stored on the **heap**. The heap is used for dynamic memory allocation, allowing data to be accessed and modified globally in your program.

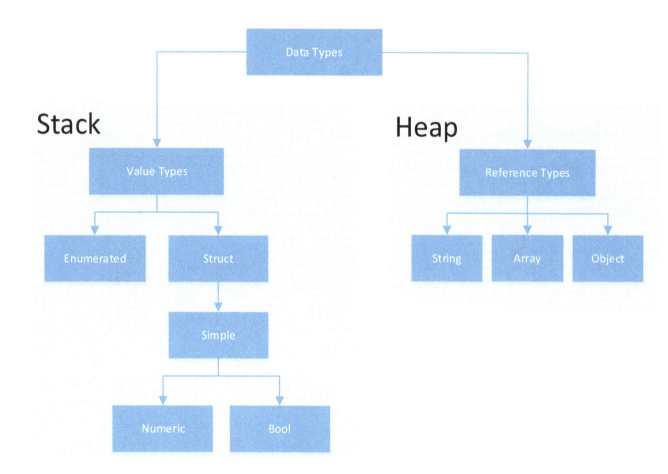

Reference types can be assigned a **null reference** using the "null" keyword, indicating that the reference points to nothing. In contrast, value types cannot be assigned null under normal circumstances.

Full Example: Memory – Stack and Heap

```csharp
int a = 7;       // Value type, stored on Stack
int b = a;       // Value type, stored on Stack
bool c = true;   // Value type, stored on Stack

string d = "Hello";    // Reference type, stored on Heap
int[] e = new int[20]; // Reference type, stored on Heap

// Instantiates an object, stored on Heap
MyClass theObject = new();
MyClass theSecondObject = theObject;

// Both objects refer to the same memory location on Heap
theObject.g = 5;
theSecondObject.g = 9;

// Output shows that modifying one reference type affects all references to that object
Console.WriteLine(theObject.g);       // Output: 9
Console.WriteLine(theSecondObject.g); // Output: 9

public class MyClass
{
        public int g { get; set; }
}
```

In this example, value types *a*, *b*, and *c* are stored on the stack, while the string *d*, array *e*, and objects *theObject* and *theSecondObject* are reference types stored on the heap. Modifying *theSecondObject.g* also changes *theObject.g* because both variables refer to the same object in the heap.

MINI QUIZ: MEMORY - HEAP AND STACK

Mini Quiz

1. An *int* is a value type.

    A. True

    B. False

2. A *string* is a value type.

    A. True

    B. False

3. An instance of a custom class is a reference type.

    A. True

    B. False

4. Local variables within a method are typically stored on the:

    A. Heap

    B. Stack

Mini Quiz Answers

1. A
2. B
3. A
4. B

MEMORY: BOXING VS UNBOXING

Boxing and **unboxing** are concepts that relate to the conversion between value types and reference types.

Boxing occurs when a value type is converted to a reference type. This involves wrapping the value type within an object on the heap. Boxing can be resource-intensive as it requires allocating memory on the heap and can increase the workload of the garbage collector.

Example: Boxing

```
int a = 123;  // Value type
object b = a; // Boxing: int value type is converted to an object (reference type)
```

Unboxing is the reverse process, where a value stored in a reference type is converted back to a value type. It requires explicit casting and can throw an *InvalidCastException* if the types do not match.

Example: Unboxing

```
int a = 123;   // Value type
object b = a;   // Boxing: int is converted to object
int c = (int)b; // Unboxing: Explicitly cast the object back to int
```

In the unboxing example, *c* is explicitly cast back to an *int*. This step is crucial as attempting to unbox to an incorrect type can result in runtime exceptions.

Understanding boxing and unboxing is important for efficient memory management and performance optimization. These operations, while sometimes necessary, can have implications for both memory usage and processing speed, and should be used carefully.

STRUCTS

A **struct** is similar to a class but is typically used for lightweight objects such as points, rectangles, and colors. Although classes can also represent these objects, using struct is often more memory-efficient since structs are value types (stored on the stack) and not reference types (stored on the heap like classes).

Example: Struct

```csharp
public struct TheLocation
{
        public int X { get; private set; }
        public int Y { get; private set; }

        // Parameterized constructor
        public TheLocation(int x, int y)
        {
                X = x;
                Y = y;
        }
}

// Using the struct
TheLocation theLocation1 = new();
Console.WriteLine($"Location1: x = {theLocation1.X}, y = {theLocation1.Y}");
// Output: Location1: x = 0, y = 0

TheLocation theLocation2 = new(23, 6);
Console.WriteLine($"Location2: x = {theLocation2.X}, y = {theLocation2.Y}");
// Output: Location2: x = 23, y = 6
```

Structs in C# have a default parameterless constructor that initializes each field to its default value. However, if a struct defines a constructor (like the parameterized constructor in the example), the default parameterless constructor is not automatically available.

A unique feature of structs is that you can declare them without using the keyword *new*. This is in contrast to classes, which always require *new* for instantiation. Note that while primitive types like *int*, *char*, and *bool* are implemented as structs in .NET, not all structs are necessarily primitive types.

Example: Declaring a Struct Without "new"

```csharp
public struct TheLocation
{
        public int X;
        public int Y;
}

// Declaring the struct without 'new'
TheLocation theLocation3;
theLocation3.X = 23;
theLocation3.Y = 6;
Console.WriteLine($"Location3: x = {theLocation3.X}, y = {theLocation3.Y}");
// Output: Location3: x = 23, y = 6
```

When using structs in collections like Lists, it's important to remember that structs are value types. This means that when a struct is added to a collection, a copy of the struct is stored in the collection. Any subsequent modifications to the original struct will not be reflected in the collection.

RECORDS

Records are designed to simplify the creation of immutable reference types and provide built-in value-based equality comparisons.

Example: Record

```
public record Student(string Name,  int Grade);
```

Example: Instantiate a Record

```
Student student1 = new("Pablo", 97);
// Immutable: properties cannot be modified after instantiation
// student1.Grade = 98; // Compile-time error
```

To create a modified copy of a record while preserving immutability, the "with" keyword is used.

Example: With Keyword

```
Student student2 = student1 with { Grade = 98 };
// Copies student1 properties, changing only Grade
```

Records provide built-in structural equality, comparing values of properties, not references.

Example: Equality

```
Student student1 = new("Pablo", 97);
Student student2 = new("Pablo", 97);
Student student3 = new("Jason", 95);
Teacher teacher1 = new("Pablo", 97);

bool match1 = student1.Equals(student2); // True
bool match2 = student1.Equals(student3); // False
bool match3 = student1.Equals(teacher1); // False, different types
```

Records support **deconstruction** into individual properties.

Example: Deconstruct

```
var (studentName, studentGrade) = student1; // Deconstruct
Console.WriteLine(studentName); // Output: Pablo
Console.WriteLine(studentGrade); // Output: 97
```

Example: Record with a Method

```
public record Student(string Name, int Grade)
{
        public void DisplayMessage()
        {
                Console.WriteLine("Hello");
        }
}
```

Example: Inheritance

```
public record ClassRoom(string Name, int Grade, int Room) : Student(Name, Grade);

ClassRoom student3 = new("Pablo", 97, 101);
student3.DisplayMessage(); // Output: Hello
```

In the inheritance example, *ClassRoom* extends *Student* by adding a new property, *Room*, while retaining the behavior of *Student*.

Example: Record Equality and Inheritance

```
Student student1 = new("Pablo", 97);
Student student2 = new("Jason",  95);

Console.WriteLine("Are student1 and student2 the same?");
Console.WriteLine(student1.Equals(student2)); // Output: false

ClassRoom student3 = new("Pablo", 97, 101);
student3.DisplayMessage(); // Output: Hello
```

NAMESPACES & USING DIRECTIVE

Namespaces are used to organize large groups of related code, helping to manage code complexity in larger projects. To use a namespace, you typically employ the **using** directive or include the namespace before the class name.

Example: Defining a Namespace

```
namespace NamespaceExample
{
        // Contents of NamespaceExample
}
```

C# 10 introduced **file-scoped namespaces** which simplifies syntax in files where all code belongs to the same namespace, reducing nesting and improving readability.

Example: File-Scoped Namespace

```
namespace NamespaceExample2Console; // Applies to the entire file
```

The *using* directive simplifies code by allowing the use of classes within a namespace without fully qualifying their names each time.

Example: Using the System Namespace

```
using System;

Console.WriteLine("Hello World!"); // Using Console class from System namespace

// Without "using System;", the full name must be used
System.Console.WriteLine("Hello World!");
```

C# 10 introduced **implicit usings**, which automatically include common namespaces. Additionally, **global usings** apply to the entire project, often placed in a *GlobalUsings.cs* file for organization.

Example: Global Using Directive

```
global using System;
```

The **using static** directive allows accessing static members of a class without specifying the class name.

Example: Using Static Directive with "System.Console"

```
using static System.Console;

WriteLine("Console.WriteLine() is simplified to just WriteLine()");
ReadLine(); // Simplified from Console.Readline()
```

Namespaces can contain multiple classes, and you can use them to organize your code logically.

Example: Namespace Created and Called

```
Console.WriteLine(Automobiles.Cars.theCar);

namespace Automobiles
{
        static class Cars
        {
                public static string theCar = "ToyotaCar";
        }

        class Trucks
        {
                // Demonstrating multiple classes in a namespace
        }
}
```

In the above example, *Automobiles.Cars.theCar* requires the full path. However, with the *using static* directive, this can be simplified.

The *using static* directive reduces verbosity for frequently accessed static members, enhancing code readability.

Example: Simplifying Access with Using Static

```
using static Automobiles.Cars;

Console.WriteLine(theCar); // Simplified from Automobiles.Cars.theCar
```

C# 12 introduced an enhancement to the using directive, expanding its aliasing capabilities. This update allows for almost any type to be aliased, including nullable value types and tuples with named elements. These enhancements offer a more flexible and powerful way to simplify code and improve readability.

Example: Extending Aliasing

```
using ProjectDictionary = System.Collections.Generic.Dictionary<int, string>;
using NullableInt = int?;
using GPSLocation = System.Tuple<double, double>;
```

GENERICS

Generics enable the creation of flexible and reusable code components that work with any data type. They allow defining type-safe data structures without committing to actual data types at the time of creation. This is especially useful in collections, as demonstrated later in the "List" section.

Generics use **type parameters**, typically enclosed in angle brackets < >, to define placeholders for the types that are specified when the class or method is instantiated. Conventionally, *T* is used as a type parameter, but other identifiers like *TKey* or *TValue* are also common.

Full Example: Defining and Using a Generic Class

```csharp
class AGenericClass<T>
{
        private T aVariable;
        public AGenericClass(T aValue)
        {
                aVariable = aValue;
                Console.WriteLine($"The value is {aVariable} and is a {typeof(T).Name}");
                // Output: "The value is Hello and is a String"
        }

        public void DisplayTypeOnly(T aValue)
        {
                Console.WriteLine($"Value {aValue}, type:  {typeof(T).Name}");
                // Output for string: "Value: Hello, type: String"
        }
}

// Instantiating with different types
AGenericClass<int> intExample = new(5); // Output: The value is 5 and is a Int32
AGenericClass<string> stringExample = new("Hello"); // Output: The value is Hello and is a String
AGenericClass<double> doubleExample = new(5.5); // Output: The value is 5.5 and is a Double

// Using the DisplayTypeOnly method
intExample.DisplayTypeOnly(5);           // Output: Value: 5, Type Int32
stringExample.DisplayTypeOnly("Hello"); // Output: Value: Hello, Type: String
doubleExample.DisplayTypeOnly(5.5);      // Output: Value: 5.5, Type: Double
```

In the above examples, the generic type parameter 'T' takes on the specific type provided at instantiation. For instance, *AGenericClass<int>* treats 'T' as an integer. This demonstrates the power of generics in creating versatile and type-safe code structures.

LISTS

Lists are flexible collections that can store a series of elements. Unlike arrays, which have a fixed size, lists can dynamically resize, making them more suitable for situations where the number of elements can change over time. They offer built-in functionalities for searching, sorting, adding, and removing items.

To use a list, the **System.Collections.Generic** namespace is typically used. With C# 10's implicit usings feature, this namespace may already be included in some project templates.

Example: Instantiate an Empty List

```csharp
List<string> foods = new();
```

Example: Traditional List Initialization

```csharp
List<string> foods = new() {"Pizza", "Burger"};
```

Example: Collection Expression

```csharp
List<string> foods = ["Pizza", "Burger"];
```

This new, concise syntax uses square brackets *[]* for initialization, introduced in C# 12's collection expressions feature.

Example: Using the Spread Operator

```csharp
List<string> moreFoods = ["Sushi", ..foods, "Taco"];
```

This combines elements from *foods* with "Sushi" and "Taco", showcasing the flexibility of C# 12 collection expressions.

Example: Assign Items to an Existing List

```csharp
foods.Add("Sushi"); // Adds "Sushi" to the list
foods.Add("Tacos"); // Adds "Tacos" to the list
```

Example: Insert at a Specific Index

```
foods.Insert(1, "Cake"); // Inserts at index 1, shifting subsequent elements
```

Example: Remove Items

```
foods.Remove("Pizza");// Removes the item "Pizza"
foods.RemoveAt(1); // Removes the item at index 1
```

Example: Access and Output Items

```
Console.WriteLine(foods[0]); // Outputs the first item
```

Example: Iterate Through a List

```
foreach (var food in foods)
{
        Console.WriteLine(food);
}
```

Example: Get List Size and Sort

```
Console.WriteLine(foods.Count); // Outputs the number of items in the list
foods.Sort();// Sorts the list alphabetically or numerically
```

Example: Clear and Convert to Array

```
foods.Clear(); // Removes all items
string[] foodsArray = foods.ToArray(); // Converts the list to an array
```

Full Example: List

```
// Instantiate and assign items to a list
List<string> foods = new() { "Pizza", "Burger", "Hot Dog" };

foods.Add("Sushi");
foods.Add("Tacos");

// Output the second item
Console.WriteLine(foods[1]); // Output: Burger

// Loop through the list and output each item
foreach (var food in foods)
{
        Console.WriteLine(food);  // Outputs Pizza, Burger, Hot Dog, Sushi, Tacos
}
```

With C# 13, working with lists becomes even more powerful due to **list patterns**. These allow you to match the structure of lists directly, making the code more readable and concise.

Example: List Patterns

```
if (foods is ["Pizza", "Burger", .., "Tacos"])
{
        Console.WriteLine("The list starts with Pizza, includes Burger, and ends with Tacos");
}
```

In this example, list patterns are used to match specific elements in a list, allowing you to check if the list starts, ends, or contains particular items without manually iterating through it.

C# 13 also introduces **relational patterns**, which are useful when working with collections that need specific condition checks. You can easily apply relational checks to items within lists.

Example: Relational Patterns with List Values

```
List<string> ages = new() { 15, 25, 30, 45 };
if (ages[1] is > 18 and < 65)
{
        Console.WriteLine("The second item in the list is a working-age adult");
}
```

These enhanced pattern matching features make working with lists and collections more expressive, reducing boilerplate code and increasing readability.

ACTIVITY: LISTS

Activity: This activity involves creating a console application for managing a grocery list. The application will allow users to add, remove, and display items from their grocery list.

1. **Prompt User Actions**: The application should display the following prompt: "Add/Remove/Display items from grocery list".

2. **Add or Remove Items**: Users should be able to add or remove as many items as they want from the grocery list.

3. **Display Grocery List**: Users should be able to display all items currently on the grocery list.

Example Output:

```
Add/Remove/Display items from grocery list: Add

What would you like to add? Chicken

Chicken has been added.

Add/Remove/Display items from grocery list: Add

Bread

Fish has been added.

Add/Remove/Display items from grocery list: Display

Grocery List:

Chicken

Fish
```

Hints:

- Use a loop, such as a while loop, to continuously prompt the user for their choice (Add, Remove, Display).

- A foreach loop can be used to iterate through and print each item in the list.

Need help with the solution? https://www.unQbd.com/Solutions/CSharp7th/List

LINKEDLIST

A **LinkedList** can be more efficient than a regular list (*List<T>*) for operations involving frequent insertions and deletions, especially in the middle of the collection. This is because, unlike a regular list, a LinkedList doesn't need to shift elements after modifications. Like lists, LinkedList also uses generics.

To use a LinkedList, you may need to add the following line of code, depending on your project setup:

```csharp
using System.Collections.Generic;
```

Example: Initializing a LinkedList

```csharp
LinkedList<string> ingredientsOrder = new();
```

Full Example: Using LinkedList and LinkedListNode

```csharp
LinkedList<string> ingredientsOrder = new();

ingredientsOrder.AddLast("Add an egg");
ingredientsOrder.AddLast("Add butter");
ingredientsOrder.AddFirst("Get a bowl");

// Find the node containing "Get a bowl"
LinkedListNode<string> node = ingredientsOrder.Find("Get a bowl");
ingredientsOrder.AddAfter(node, "Add sugar");

foreach (string item in ingredientsOrder)
{
        Console.WriteLine(item);
        // Output: Get a bowl
        // Output: Add sugar
        // Output: Add an egg
        // Output: Add butter
}
```

In this example, *LinkedListNode* is used to reference specific elements in the *LinkedList*, allowing for more precise control over the list's structure. It's important to note that while *LinkedList* excels in certain operations, accessing elements by index can be slower due to the need for sequential traversal.

DICTIONARY

Dictionaries are collections that store elements in **key-value** pairs, allowing for fast retrieval based on the key. Unlike arrays, where keys (indexes) are automatically assigned, dictionaries allow for meaningful and unique key names. Like lists, dictionaries use generics.

To use a dictionary, you typically include this line: *using System.Collections.Generic*; (Note: With C# 10's implicit usings feature, this namespace may already be included in your project.)

Dictionaries have two generic type parameters: one for the **key** and one for the **value**. These can be any types. Below, a *string* is used for the key and an *int* for the value.

Example: Instantiate a Dictionary

```
Dictionary<string, int> myInventory = new();
```

Example: Assign Items

```
myInventory.Add("Pens", 7);
myInventory.Add("Computers", 2);
```

Example: Instantiate and Assign Items

```
Dictionary<string, int> myInventory = new()
{
        { "Pens", 7 },
        { "Computers", 2 }
};
```

Example: Remove Items

```
myInventory.Remove("Pens");
```

Example: Update an Item

```
myInventory["Computers"] = 6;
```

Example: Output an Item

```
int computerCount = myInventory["Computers"];
Console.WriteLine($"Computers: {computerCount}");
```

Example: Loop Through a Dictionary

```
foreach (KeyValuePair<string, int> item in myInventory)
{
        Console.WriteLine($"{item.Key}: quantity {item.Value} ");
}
```

This loop uses **KeyValuePair<TKey, TValue>** because each element in the dictionary is a key-value pair.

Example: Get Dictionary Size

```
Console.WriteLine(myInventory.Count);
```

Example: Clear a Dictionary

```
myInventory.Clear();
```

Full Example: Dictionary

```
Dictionary<string, int> myInventory = new()
{
        { "Pens", 7 },
        { "Computers", 2 }
};
// Outputs the quantity of pens
Console.WriteLine(myInventory["Pens"]); // Output: 7

// Loop through the dictionary and output each item
foreach (KeyValuePair<string, int> item in myInventory)
{
        Console.WriteLine($"{item.Key}: quantity {item.Value} ");
}
// Outputs
// Pens: quantity 7
// Computers: quantity 2
```

ENUMERATION

An **enum** (enumeration) is a value type that defines a set of **named constants**. Enums enhance code clarity, type safety, and reduce the likelihood of invalid constants. Typically, enums are defined directly in the namespace, outside of any class, and are backed by an integral type, defaulting to *int*.

Example: Declare an Enum

```
enum Direction { North, East, South, West };
```

Enums improve readability and ensure type safety. The *ToString* method is implicitly used when an enum is output.

Example: Assign and Output an Enum Value

```
Direction PlayerDirection = Direction.North;
Console.WriteLine(PlayerDirection); // Output: North
```

Using enums in conditional statements enhances clarity.

Example: Enum in Conditional Statements

```
if (PlayerDirection == Direction.North)
{
        Console.WriteLine("The player heads north");
}
else if (PlayerDirection == Direction.East)
{
        Console.WriteLine("The player heads east into the woods.");
}
```

Iterating over enums with *foreach* is straightforward, using *Enum.GetValues*.

Example: Enum in a Loop

```
foreach (Direction direction in Enum.GetValues(typeof(Direction)))
{
        Console.WriteLine(direction);
}
```

This example demonstrates a class using enums in various contexts. It illustrates changing enum values and checking them in conditional logic.

Full Example: Using Enums

```csharp
// Enum declaration
enum Direction { North, East, South, West };

// Class that uses the enum
class EnumExample
{
        private Direction PlayerDirection = Direction.North;

        public void Directions()
        {
                // Output all enum values
                Console.Write("You can go the following directions: ");
                foreach (Direction direction in Enum.GetValues(typeof(Direction)))
                {
                        Console.Write($"{direction} ");
                }
                Console.WriteLine();

                // Change the PlayerDirection for demonstration
                PlayerDirection = Direction.East;

                if (PlayerDirection == Direction.North)
                {
                        Console.WriteLine("The player heads north");
                }
                else if (PlayerDirection == Direction.East)
                {
                        Console.WriteLine("The player heads east into the woods.");
                }
        }
}

// Create an instance of the class and call the method
EnumExample display = new();
display.Directions();
```

Assigning specific values to enums can be useful for clarity or external system compatibility.

Example: Enum with Assigned Values

```
enum Month { January = 1, February = 2, March = 3, April = 4, May = 5 }; // and so on …

public static void MonthNumber()
{
        Month value = Month.February;
        int monthNumber = (int)value;
        Console.WriteLine(monthNumber); // Output: 2
}
```

MINI QUIZ: ENUMERATION

Mini Quiz

1. Enums are typically defined outside of any class, directly in the namespace

    A. True

    B. False

2. Is the following enum declaration valid?

```
enum Size { Small, Medium, Large, Extra Large, XXL };
```

    A. True

    B. False

3. Enums are used to enhance code clarity and reduce the risk of introducing invalid constants

    A. True

    B. False

4. Can enum members be explicitly assigned integer values as shown in the example below?

```
enum Rating { Horrible = 1, OK = 2, Good = 3, Great = 4, Amazing = 5 };
```

    A. True

    B. False

Mini Quiz Answers

1. B
2. B – "Extra Large" must be 1 word with no spacing "ExtraLarge"
3. A
4. A

TERNARY OPERATOR

The **ternary** operator is a concise way to evaluate a condition and return one of two values depending on the outcome of that condition. It can often simplify traditional "If-Else" statements.

Ternary Format:

```
Condition ? First_Result : Second_Result
```

Example: Ternary Operator

```
int timeOfDay = 10;
string morningOrNight = (timeOfDay < 12) ? "Morning" : "Night"; // Morning is assigned
```

This example demonstrates the simplification provided by the ternary operator compared to a traditional "If-Else" statement.

Example: "If-Else" Statement vs Ternary Operator

```
int myAge = 23;
string theResponse;

// If-Else statement example
if (myAge < 21)
{
        theResponse = "Under 21 years old";
}
else
{
        theResponse = "Over 21 years old";
}
Console.WriteLine(theResponse); // Output: Over 21 years old

// Ternary operator example
theResponse = (myAge < 21) ? "Under 21 years old" : "Over 21 years old";

Console.WriteLine(theResponse); // Output: Over 21 years old
```

Example: Ternary Operator in a Method

```
Console.WriteLine(AgeCheck(19)); // Output: Under 21 years old
static string AgeCheck(int theAge)
{
        return (theAge < 21) ? "Under 21 years old" : "Over 21 years old";
}
```

DATETIME

DateTime is a struct that is used to represent an instant in time, including both the date and the time of day.

Example: Assign Current Date/Time with 'Now'

```
DateTime todaysDate = DateTime.Now;
Console.WriteLine(todaysDate); // Output: will vary based on your current date/time
```

Example: Create a Specific Date

```
DateTime dob = new DateTime(1984, 1, 20); // (Year, Month, Day)
Console.WriteLine(dob);  // Output: 1/20/1984 12:00:00 AM
```

Example: Create a Specific Date and Time

```
DateTime dob = new DateTime(1984, 1, 20, 2, 30, 5); // (Year, Month, Day, Hour, Minute, Second)
Console.WriteLine(dob);  // Output: 1/20/1984 2:30:05 AM
```

You can format the date and time in various ways using standard format specifiers:

Example: Formatting Date and Time

```
DateTime dob = new(1984, 1, 20, 2, 30, 5);
Console.WriteLine($"The Month is: {dob.Month}");       // Output: 1
Console.WriteLine($"The Month is: {dob:MM}");          // Output: 01
Console.WriteLine($"The Month is: {dob:MMM}");         // Output: Jan
Console.WriteLine($"The Month is: {dob:MMMM}");        // Output: January
Console.WriteLine($"The date is: {dob.Day}");          // Output: 20
Console.WriteLine($"The date is: {dob:d}");            // Output: 01/20/1984
Console.WriteLine($"The date is: {dob:D}");            // Output: Friday, January 20, 1984
Console.WriteLine($"The time is: {dob.TimeOfDay}");    // Output: 02:30:05
Console.WriteLine($"The time is: {dob:H:mm}");         // Output: 2:30
Console.WriteLine($"The time is: {dob:H:mm tt}");      // Output: 2:30 AM
```

Once a DateTime object is created, there are ways to add and subtract time from it. In the example below, a month is added using *AddMonths*.

Example: Add Time

```
DateTime dob = new(1984, 1, 20, 2, 30, 5);

DateTime addMonthToDOB = dob.AddMonths(1);
Console.WriteLine($"The Month: {addMonthToDOB.Month}"); // Output: The Month: 2
```

DateTime objects can be compared using the *Compare* method or operators:

Example: Comparing DateTime Objects

```
DateTime firstDate = new(2022, 1, 23);
DateTime secondDate = new(2023, 1, 23);

int result = DateTime.Compare(firstDate, secondDate);

if (result < 0)
{
        Console.WriteLine("The first date is earlier");
}
else if (result > 0)
{
        Console.WriteLine("The first date is later");
}
else
{
        Console.WriteLine("The dates are the same");
}

// Direct comparison using operators
if (firstDate < secondDate)
{
        Console.WriteLine("The first date is earlier");
}
```

ACTIVITY: DATETIME

Activity: Create a Console Application to determine the day of the week you were born.

1. **Gather User Input:**

   - Prompt the user with the following questions:

     - "What year were you born?" (expect a numeric value)

     - "What month were you born?" (accept either a numeric value or month name)

     - "What day were you born?" (expect a numeric value)

2. **Create a DateTime Object:**

   - Use the user's answers to create a **DateTime** object representing their birth date.

3. **Display the Day of Week:**

   - Output the day of the week on which the user was born.

Example Output:

```
What year were you born? 1990

What month were you born? 5

What day were you born? 15

You were born on a Tuesday.
```

Hints:

- Use the **DayOfWeek** property of the **DateTime** object to get the day of the week.

- Consider using **TryParse** methods for more robust error handling.

Need help with the solution? https://www.unQbd.com/Solutions/CSharp7th/DateTime

THIS (REFERENCE)

The **this** keyword is used to refer to the current instance of the class. It is primarily used to distinguish between class members and parameters or local variables with the same name. Additionally, *this* can pass the entire instance of the current class to a method as an object.

Example: *this* for Member Reference

```csharp
private string name = "Adam";
public void DisplayName(string name)
{
        Console.WriteLine(this.name); // Output: Adam
        Console.WriteLine(name);      // Output: Parameter value
}
```

In this example, *this.name* refers to the class member, while *name* refers to the method's parameter.

Full Example: Passing *this* to a Method

```csharp
class NameClass
{
        private string name = "Adam";
        public string FirstName { get; set; } = "Samantha";
        public string LastName { get; set; } = "West";

        public void DisplayName(string name)
        {
                Console.WriteLine(this.name);                      // Output: Adam
                Console.WriteLine(name);                           // Output: Parameter value
                Console.WriteLine(NameHelp.CombineName(this)); // Passes current instance
        }
}
static class NameHelp
{
        public static string CombineName(NameClass nameClass)
        {
                return $"{nameClass.FirstName} {nameClass.LastName}"; // Output: Samantha West
        }
}
```

Here, *NameHelp.CombineName(this)* demonstrates passing the entire instance of *NameClass* to the *CombineName* method.

METHODS: EXTENSION

Extension methods enable the addition of new methods to existing types without altering the type's source code or creating a new derived type. These methods are static methods defined in static classes but are called as if they were instance methods on the extended type.

Example: Creating an Extension Method

```csharp
public static class StringExtensions
{
        public static void ToStarBox(this string text)
        {
                string starLine = new string('*', text.Length + 2);

                Console.WriteLine(starLine);
                Console.WriteLine($"*{text}*");
                Console.WriteLine(starLine);
        }
}
```

Here, *ToStarBox* is an extension method for the *string* type. Notice how it uses the *this* keyword to specify the type it extends.

Example: Call an Extension Method

```csharp
string aWord = "Hello";

aWord.ToStarBox();
// Output:
// *******
// *Hello*
// *******
```

In this example, *ToStarBox* is called on a **string** object as if it were a built-in method of the *string* class.

Full Example: Extension Method Usage

```csharp
// In a separate static class
public static class StringExtensions
{
        public static void ToStarBox(this string text)
        {
                string starLine = new string('*', text.Length + 2);

                Console.WriteLine(starLine);
                Console.WriteLine($"*{text}*");
                Console.WriteLine(starLine);
        }
}

// Usage
string aWord = "Hello";
aWord.ToStarBox();
// Output:
// *******
// *Hello*
// *******
```

This full example demonstrates how the *ToStarBox* extension method can be seamlessly integrated and used like a native method of the *string* class.

ACTIVITY: METHODS - EXTENSION

Activity: This activity involves creating a Console Application named "Lucky Number App". The goal is to use an extension method to determine if a number is considered lucky. In this activity, define the numbers 7 and 13 as lucky.

1. **Display a Prompt**: The application should display the prompt: "Enter a number to find out if it is lucky: ".

2. **Create an Extension Method**: Implement an extension method for the **int** type. This method should return the string "Lucky" if the number is 7 or 13, and "Not Lucky" otherwise.

3. **Display the Result**: After the user enters a number, the application should display whether the number is lucky or not.

Example Output:

For a user entering 7, the output should be:

```
Enter a number to find out if it is lucky: 7

Lucky
```

For a user entering 5, the output should be:

```
Enter a number to find out if it is lucky: 5

Not Lucky
```

Hints:

- Define a static class for your extension method.

- Your extension method should have one parameter of type *int*, prefixed with the *this* keyword.

- Call the extension method on an *int* instance to determine if it is lucky.

Need help with the solution? https://www.unQbd.com/Solutions/CSharp7th/ExtensionMethod

TUPLES

A **tuple** can be thought of as a lightweight data structure similar to an array, with the key difference that a tuple can contain elements of different data types. Tuples are often used for returning multiple values from a method.

There are two tuple types:

Classic Tuples (Tuple type): They are generic containers that can hold between 1 to 8 items. For more than 8 items, nested tuples are used.

Example: Instantiate and Access a Classic Tuple

```csharp
// Instantiate a tuple
Tuple<int, string, int[]> myTuple = Tuple.Create(101, "Hello", new int[] { 41, 52 });

// Access Tuple elements
Console.WriteLine(myTuple.Item1); // Output: 101
Console.WriteLine(myTuple.Item2); // Output: Hello

foreach (int number in myTuple.Item3)
{
        Console.Write($"{number} "); // Output 41 52
}
```

Value Tuples (ValueTuple type): ValueTuples are more flexible and performant. They allow for element naming and are generally preferred over classic tuples.

Example: Using ValueTuple

```csharp
// Instantiate a ValueTuple
var myValueTuple = (Id: 101, Greeting: "Hello", Numbers: new int[] { 41, 52 });

// Access ValueTuple elements
Console.WriteLine(myValueTuple.Id); // Output: 101
Console.WriteLine(myValueTuple.Greeting); // Output: Hello

foreach (int number in myValueTuple.Numbers)
{
        Console.Write($"{number} "); // Output 41 52
}
```

Tuples are particularly useful for returning multiple values from a method.

Example: Tuple in a Method

```
int num1 = 10;
int num2 = 4;

// Using tuple deconstruction
(var quotient, var remainder) = DivideGetQuotientAndRemainder(num1, num2);
Console.WriteLine($"{num1} / {num2} = {quotient}, with remainder of {remainder}");
// Output: 10 / 4 = 2, with remainder of 2

static (int quotient, int remainder) DivideGetQuotientAndRemainder(int dividend, int divisor)
{
        int quotient = dividend / divisor;
        int remainder = dividend % divisor; // Uses modulus operator (%) to get remainder

        return (quotient, remainder);
}
```

Tuple deconstruction is a feature that allows for the unpacking of tuple elements into separate variables. In the example above, the method *DivideGetQuotientAndRemainder* returns a tuple containing two elements (quotient and remainder). These elements are then unpacked into two separate variables (*quotient* and *remainder*) using tuple deconstruction. This feature simplifies the process of working with tuples, making the code more readable and concise.

MINI QUIZ: TUPLES

Mini Quiz

1. What is the maximum number of elements a Classic Tuple can hold directly?

    A. 7
    B. 8
    C. 9
    D. Unlimited

2. A Tuple can hold any data type.

    A. True
    B. False

3. Which of the following correctly creates a ValueTuple?

    A. var myValueTuple = (101, "Hello", new int[] { 41, 52 });

    B. ValueTuple<int, string, int[]> myValueTuple = (101, "Hello", new int[] { 41, 52 });

    C. Tuple<int, string, int[]> myValueTuple = Tuple.Create(101, "Hello", new int[] { 41, 52 });

    D. var myValueTuple = ValueTuple.Create(101, "Hello", new int[] { 41, 52 });

4. How do you access the second element of a Classic Tuple Tuple<int, string>?

    A. Item2

    B. Element2

    C. Second

    D. None of the above

Mini Quiz Answers

1. B
2. A
3. A
4. A

STRINGBUILDER

Strings are **immutable**, meaning they cannot be changed once created. When a string is modified, a new string object is created in memory, which can lead to additional system resource usage, especially in cases of frequent modifications. **StringBuilder**, part of the *System.Text* namespace, is a **mutable** string-like object designed to overcome this limitation. Its value can be changed without creating a new string object in memory each time it is modified.

To use *StringBuilder*, include the using statement:

```csharp
using System.Text;
```

Example: Instantiate a StringBuilder

```csharp
StringBuilder theBuilder = new("Hello World!");
```

Example: Append to a StringBuilder

```csharp
// Appends new content at the end of the existing string
StringBuilder theBuilder = new("Hello World!");
theBuilder.Append(" Today is going to be great!");
Console.WriteLine(theBuilder); // Output: "Hello World! Today is going to be great!
```

Example: Insert into a StringBuilder

```csharp
// Inserts content at a specified index
StringBuilder theBuilder = new("Hello how are you?");
theBuilder.Insert(5, " Jason,");
Console.WriteLine(theBuilder); // Output: "Hello Jason, how are you?
```

Example: Removes from a StringBuilder

```csharp
// Removes content starting from a specified index and for a specified length
StringBuilder theBuilder = new("Hello how are you?");
theBuilder.Remove(5, 13);
Console.WriteLine(theBuilder); // Output: "Hello"
```

Example: Replace Part of a StringBuilder

```
// Replaces a specified substring with another string
StringBuilder theBuilder = new("Hello, how are you?");
theBuilder.Replace("Hello", "Jason");
Console.WriteLine(theBuilder); // Output: "Jason, how are you?"
```

Example: Replace the Entire String in StringBuilder

```
// To replace the entire content, it's more efficient to clear and then append new text
StringBuilder theBuilder = new("Hello, how are you?");
theBuilder.Clear();
theBuilder.Append("Completely new text");
Console.WriteLine(theBuilder); // Output: "Completely new text."
```

Full Example: Using StringBuilder

```
// Full example demonstrating various StringBuilder operations
using System.Text;

StringBuilder theBuilder = new("Hello World!");

// Append text
theBuilder.Append(" Today is going to be great!");
Console.WriteLine(theBuilder); // Output: Hello World! Today is going to be great!

// Replace a part of the string
theBuilder.Replace("World", "Jason");
Console.WriteLine(theBuilder); // Output: Hello Jason! Today is going to be great!

// Replace the entire content
theBuilder.Clear();
theBuilder.Append("Completely new text");
Console.WriteLine(theBuilder); // Output: "Completely new text."
```

MINI QUIZ: STRINGBUILDER

Mini Quiz

1. StringBuilder is mutable.

    A. True
    B. False

2. When the value of a string is assigned a new value, the string object in memory is updated with the new information.

    A. True
    B. False

3. The following code would create a StringBuilder:

```
StringBuilder reply = "message";
```

    A. True
    B. False

4. Would it be better to use a String or StringBuilder for text that is going to be changed 1,000 times?

    A. String
    B. StringBuilder

5. Which method is used to remove a specified length of characters from a StringBuilder starting at a given index?

    A. Append()
    B. Insert()
    C. Remove()
    D. Replace()

Mini Quiz Answers

1. A
2. B
3. B
4. B – A string would use additional memory resources.
5. C

TRY-CATCH

Try-Catch is essential for managing unexpected conditions or errors, known as **exceptions**. Exception handling ensures that when an error occurs, the program can gracefully divert to a **catch** block, enhancing stability and reliability. This mechanism allows for a controlled response, like error logging or user notification, without stopping the entire program.

Example: Try-Catch

```
try
{
        // Code that could potentially cause an exception
}
catch (OverflowException ex)
{
        // Handle specific exceptions first, such as OverflowException
}
catch (Exception ex)
{
        // General exception handling
}
```

Optionally, a **finally** block can be added to the Try-Catch structure. This block executes regardless of whether an exception occurred, making it ideal for resource cleanup and ensuring that resources like file handles or network connections are properly closed.

Example: Finally and Multiple Catches

```
try
{
        // Code that might throw an exception
}
catch (OverflowException ex)
{
        // Handle specific exceptions first, such as OverflowException
}
catch (Exception ex)
{
        // Handle all other exceptions
}
finally
{
        // Code here always executes, ideal for cleanup
}
```

In practical applications, it's common to handle input-related exceptions. The following example demonstrates handling exceptions when parsing user input into dates:

Example: Handling Input Exceptions

```csharp
try
{
        Console.WriteLine("Enter a day between 1 to 31");
        int theDay = int.Parse(Console.ReadLine());

        Console.WriteLine("Enter a month between 1 to 12");
        int theMonth = int.Parse(Console.ReadLine());

        Console.WriteLine("Enter a 4-digit year");
        int theYear = int.Parse(Console.ReadLine());

        DateTime dt = new(theYear, theMonth, theDay);
        Console.WriteLine($"Formatted Date: {dt:dddd, MMM d, yyyy}");
}
catch (FormatException ex)
{
        Console.WriteLine($"Input Format Exception: {ex.Message}");
}
catch (Exception ex)
{
        Console.WriteLine($"General Exception: {ex.Message}");
}
finally
{
        // Code for cleanup or final operations
}
```

MINI QUIZ: TRY-CATCH

Mini Quiz

1. There can be multiple Finally blocks in a Try.

    A. True
    B. False

2. The most generic Catch block should go last.

    A. True
    B. False

3. The Finally block only executes if there is an exception.

    A. True
    B. False

4. The Finally block is required in a Try-Catch structure.

    A. True
    B. False

5. The following code will catch all exceptions.

```
catch (Exception ex)
{
        // Handle exception
}
```

    A. True
    B. False

Mini Quiz Answers

5. A
4. B
3. B
2. A
1. B

UNIT TESTING

Unit Tests are essential in verifying that the logic of code is working as expected. They break down a program into small, testable units to ensure each part functions correctly.

Walkthrough: Setting up a .NET Console Application xUnit Test

The objective is to build a calculator that adds two numbers and validate its functionality using unit testing.

1. **Create a Console Application**: Name it *UTCalculator*.

2.

2. **Create a Class**: Name it *CalculatorFeatures* with a method *AddTwoNumbers*. Note: Initially, we'll introduce an intentional error here for demonstration purposes.

```csharp
namespace UTCalculator
{
    public class CalculatorFeatures
    {
        public static int AddTwoNumbers(int num1, int num2)
        {
            // Intentional error for demonstration
            int result = num1 - num2;
            return result;
        }
    }
}
```

3. **Test the Method Manually**: Add a *Console.WriteLine* to test the method.

```
Console.WriteLine(UTCalculator.CalculatorFeatures.AddTwoNumbers(10, 4)); // Incorrect Output: 6
```

This should output 14, but due to the logic error, it will incorrectly output 6.

4. **Set Up the xUnit Test Project**:

- Right-click on the Solution in Solution Explorer.

- Click on Add, then New Project.

- Choose xUnit Test Project (.NET Core) and name it **CalculatorTest**.

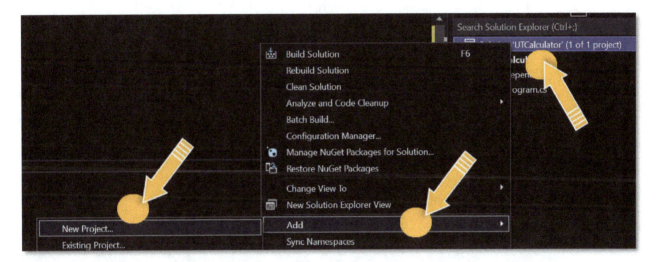

5. **Add a Project Reference**:

- In *CalculatorTest*, right-click on Dependencies.

- Click Add Project Reference and select *UTCalculator*.

6. **Write the Unit Test**:

- Add the *using UTCalculator;* declaration.

- Write a test method named *TestAddMethodResultShouldBeNine* using *[Fact]*.

```csharp
using Xunit;
using UTCalculator;

namespace CalculatorTest
{
    public class UnitTest1
    {
        [Fact]
        public void TestAddMethodResultShouldBeNine()
        {
            int result = CalculatorFeatures.AddTwoNumbers(5, 4);
            Assert.Equal(9, result); // Asserts that the result should be 9
        }
    }
}
```

7. **Run the Test**:

- Go to Test -> Run All Tests.
- The test will fail, showing "Expected: 9 Actual: 1", indicating the logical error.

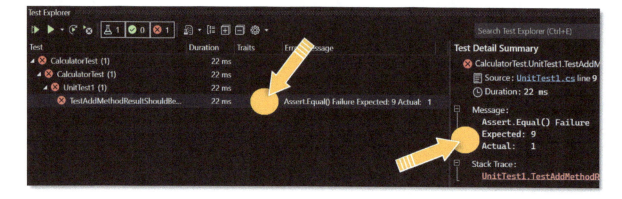

8. **Fix the Error**:

- In *CalculatorFeatures*, change the minus sign to a plus.

```
public class CalculatorFeatures
{
        public static int AddTwoNumbers(int num1, int num2)
        {
                int result = num1 + num2;
                return result;
        }
}
```

9. **Re-run the Test**: Now, all tests should pass, confirming the method works correctly.

Unit testing is a crucial part of software development, helping to catch errors early and ensuring that individual parts of the program work as intended. This example demonstrates how xUnit can be used in .NET applications to validate code functionality effectively.

In xUnit tests, tests are either marked with the attribute **[Fact]** or **[Theory]**. The *[Fact]* attribute denotes a test that does not require any external data or parameters. In contrast, *[Theory]* allows for testing the same unit test method with multiple sets of data, using *[InlineData]* to specify each set.

In our previous walkthrough, we used the **Assert** class to compare expected and actual results. This class contains various methods that return a boolean result. Here, we focus on using **Assert.Equal**.

Below is the class and method corresponding to our xUnit test, as used in the Unit Testing walkthrough:

```csharp
public class CalculatorFeatures
{
        public static int AddTwoNumbers(int num1, int num2)
        {
                int result = num1 + num2;
                return result;
        }
}
```

Example: Fact with Assert.Equal

```csharp
[Fact]
public void TestAddMethodResultShouldBeNine()
{
        int result = CalculatorFeatures.AddTwoNumbers(5, 4);
        Assert.Equal(9, result);
}
```

[Theory] allows us to test multiple scenarios in a single test method. The *[InlineData]* attributes provide different sets of inputs for each test run.

Example: Theory – Assert.Equal

```
[Theory]
[InlineData(5, 4, 9)]
[InlineData(6, 1, 7)]
[InlineData(2, 3, 5)]
public void AddTwoNumbersAndGetResult(int firstNum, int secondNum, int expectedResult)
{
        int result = CalculatorFeatures.AddTwoNumbers(firstNum, secondNum);
        Assert.Equal(expectedResult, result);
}
```

This approach to unit testing, particularly with **[Theory]** and **[InlineData]**, enables thorough testing of methods across a range of input conditions, enhancing the robustness of the code.

DIRECTIVES

Preprocessor directives are used to enhance code readability, reduce complexity, and aid in maintenance. Each directive serves a specific purpose, such as conditional compilation, emitting custom warnings or errors, and organizing code.

The **#region** and **#endregion** directives are used to define a collapsible block of code, which helps in organizing and managing large code files in Visual Studio.

Example: #region and #endregion Directives

```
#region DisplayPrompts
Console.WriteLine("Hello");
Console.WriteLine("World");
#endregion
```

The **#define** directive is placed at the top of the code file and is used to declare conditional compilation symbols.

Example: #define, #if, #else, and #endif #define

```
#define DevMode

string myDatabase = "";

#if (DevMode)
        Console.WriteLine("In development Mode, using local database");
        myDatabase = "C:\\LocalDatabase...";
#else
        Console.WriteLine("In production Mode, using remote database");
        myDatabase = "C:\\RemoteDatabase...";
#endif
```

In this example, the *#else* section is compiled only when *DevMode* is not defined.

List of Preprocessor Directives:

- **Conditional Compilation**: #if, #else, #elif, #endif, #define, #undef

- **Others**: #warning, #error, #line, #region, #endregion, #pragma, #pragma warning, #pragma checksum

Each directive serves a specific purpose:

- **#if**, **#else**, **#elif**, **#endif**: Used for conditional compilation.

- **#define**, **#undef**: Define and undefine conditional compilation symbols.

- **#warning**, **#error**: Emit custom warnings and errors during compilation.

- **#line**: Modify the compiler's line number and file information.

- **#region**, **#endregion**: Mark a block of code for organization.

- **#pragma**: Provide compiler-specific instructions, particularly for disabling certain warnings.

Preprocessor directives are powerful tools for managing different aspects of code compilation and readability, especially in complex projects.

WRITING/READING TEXT FILES

Data stored in variables is temporary and lost once the program terminates. Writing to and reading from text files is a way to handle data persistently.

The **StreamWriter** and **StreamReader** classes, part of the *System.IO* namespace, are used for writing to and reading from text files, respectively. Starting with C# 10, the Implicit Usings feature can automatically include common namespaces like *System.IO* in certain project types if enabled.

Example: Write text to a file; The file will be located in the project's output directory unless an absolute path is specified.

```csharp
string fileName = "test.txt";
string textToAdd = "Example text to save";

using (StreamWriter writer = new(fileName, true)) // 'true' to append if file exists
{
        writer.Write(textToAdd);
}
```

The *using* statement ensures that *StreamWriter* is disposed of correctly, releasing the file handle.

The ability to read from this file is also needed, and for that use *StreamReader*, which is set up with a very similar syntax to *StreamWriter*.

Example: Reading from a file can be done line by line or by reading the entire content.

```csharp
// Read one line
using (StreamReader reader = new(fileName))
{
        string onlyOneLine = reader.ReadLine();
        Console.WriteLine(onlyOneLine);
}

// Read the entire file
using (StreamReader reader = new(fileName))
{
        string wholeTextfile = reader.ReadToEnd();
        Console.WriteLine(wholeTextfile);
}
```

INTERFACES

An **interface** acts as a contract, defining a set of methods and properties that implementing classes must provide. Interface members are implicitly abstract and public, and interfaces typically start with a capital "I" as per convention. They cannot contain data fields or define constructors.

Example: Interface

```csharp
interface IPets
{
        void Greeting();
        string Name { get; set; }
}

public class Cat : IPets
{
        public string Name { get; set; }

        public void Greeting()
        {
                Console.WriteLine($"Hello cat named {Name}");
        }
}
```

The *Cat* class must implement both the *Greeting* method and *Name* property from *IPets*.

C# supports implementing multiple interfaces in a class. If a class inherits from a base class and interfaces, the base class must be listed first.

Example: Multiple Interfaces and Base Class

```csharp
public class DeckOfCards : ABaseClass, IInterface, IInterface2
{
        // Implementation details
}
```

Example: Interface

```csharp
interface IFood
{
        void Prepare();
}

public class Cake : IFood
{
        public void Prepare()
        {
                Console.WriteLine("Bake cake 20 mins");
                Console.WriteLine("Frost Cake");
        }
}

public class Pasta : IFood
{
        public void Prepare()
        {
                Console.WriteLine("Boil pasta for 12 minutes");
                Console.WriteLine("Strain water and add sauce");
        }
}


var foodList = new List<IFood> { new Cake(), new Pasta() };

foreach (IFood food in foodList)
{
        food.Prepare();
}
```

This example shows how different classes can implement the same interface, demonstrating polymorphism.

Full Example: IEnumerable and IEnumerator

```csharp
using System.Collections;

class DeckOfCards : IEnumerable
{
        private List<Card> deckList = new();

        public DeckOfCards()
        {
                deckList.Add(new Card("Two", 2, "Spade"));
                deckList.Add(new Card("Three", 3, "Spade"));
                deckList.Add(new Card("Four", 4, "Spade"));
        }

        public IEnumerator GetEnumerator()
        {
                return deckList.GetEnumerator();
        }
}

class Card
{
        public string Name { get; set; }
        public int Value { get; set; }
        public string Suit { get; set; }

        public Card(string name, int value, string suit)
        {
                Name = name; Value = value; Suit = suit;
        }
}

// Usage
DeckOfCards theDeck = new();
foreach (Card card in theDeck)
{
        Console.WriteLine($"Card: {card.Suit} {card.Name} ({card.Value})");
}
```

Here, *DeckOfCards* implements *IEnumerable*, allowing it to be iterated over using a foreach loop.

Commonly used interfaces include *IEnumerable*, *IList*, *IDictionary*, and *IComparable*. *IEnumerable* allows a class to be iterated over and requires the implementation of *IEnumerator*. *IList* provides methods for collections that can be individually accessed by index, among others.

MINI QUIZ: INTERFACES

Mini Quiz

1. Can a class inherit from multiple interfaces?

    A. True

    B. False

2. Is the following code valid in C#?

```csharp
public class ExampleClass : IInterfaceOne, IInterfaceTwo, ABaseClass
{
   // Empty class
}
```

    A. True

    B. False

3. Must classes that inherit from an interface implement all of the interface's members?

    A. True

    B. False

4. Can a List store instances of an interface type?

    A. True

    B. False

Mini Quiz Answers

1. A
2. B – The two interfaces must be after the class "ABaseClass"
3. A
4. A

YIELD

The **yield** keyword is used in implementing iterators, specifically with *IEnumerable*. The **yield return** statement is used to provide a value to the enumerator object or to signal the end of iteration using **yield break**.

This example demonstrates using *yield* in an iterator method to selectively return elements from a list, stopping when a certain condition is met.

Full Example: Using Yield Return and Yield Break

```csharp
Console.WriteLine("Output all numbers greater than 5, stop if number is 7");

List<int> myNumbers = new() { 9, 4, 20, 3, 7, 12 };

foreach (int item in GreaterThan5StopIf7())
{
        Console.Write($"{item} "); // Output: 9 20
}

IEnumerable<int> GreaterThan5StopIf7()
{
        foreach (int item in myNumbers)
        {
                if (item == 7)
                {
                        yield break;        // End iteration
                }
                else if (item > 5)
                {
                        yield return item; // Return element and continue iteration
                }
        }
}
```

In this example, the *GreaterThan5StopIf7* method iterates over each element in *myNumbers*. If an element is greater than 5, it is returned to the caller. The iteration stops if an element with the value 7 is encountered, using *yield break*.

DELEGATES

Delegates are a fundamental feature that allow you to treat methods as variables. They are type-safe, meaning they can store references to methods with a specific signature (parameter and return types). This allows methods to be passed as parameters, stored in collections, or used as event handlers, providing a high degree of flexibility in your code.

Example: Create a Delegate

```
public delegate string MathExample(int num1, int num2);
```

This delegate can hold references to any method that takes two integers as input and returns a string.

Here, we define two methods, *AddNumbers* and *MultiplyNumbers*, and demonstrate how to use them with the *MathExample* delegate.

Example: Use a Delegate

```
int number1 = 3;
int number2 = 7;

MathExample calculateMath = AddNumbers; // Store the AddNumbers method in the delegate
Console.WriteLine(calculateMath(number1, number2)); // Output: 3 + 7 = 10

static string AddNumbers(int a, int b)
{
        return $"{a} + {b} = {a + b}";
}
```

In this example, the *calculateMath* delegate holds the *AddNumbers* method and executes it with the specified arguments.

An array of delegates demonstrates the flexibility of storing and executing multiple methods.

Full Example: Array of Delegates

```csharp
public delegate string MathExample(int num1, int num2);

int number1 = 3;
int number2 = 7;

// Declare and instantiate an array of MathExample delegates
MathExample[] mathOperations = { AddNumbers, MultiplyNumbers };


foreach (var mathOperation in mathOperations)
{
        Console.WriteLine(mathOperation(number1, number2));
        // Outputs:
        // 3 + 7 = 10
        // 3 * 7 = 21
}

static string AddNumbers(int a, int b)
{
        return $"{a} + {b} = {a + b}";
}

static string MultiplyNumbers(int a, int b)
{
        return $"{a} * {b} = {a * b}";
}
```

In this full example, an array of *MathExample* delegates is created, each storing a different mathematical operation. The *public delegate string MathExample(int num1, int num2);* line defines the delegate, which is then used to store references to the *AddNumbers* and *MultiplyNumbers* methods. This example illustrates how delegates can be used effectively to store and execute multiple methods.

MINI QUIZ: DELEGATES

Mini Quiz

1. A delegate can store a method.

    A. True
    B. False

2. The following code is valid way to declare a delegate.

```
public delegate int Word(string text);
```

    A. True
    B. False

3. You can store a delegate in an array.

    A. True
    B. False

4. When creating a delegate there can be only one parameter.

    A. True
    B. False

5. Which of the following statements is true about delegates?

    A. Delegates can only reference methods that return void.
    B. Delegates are not type-safe.
    C. Delegates can store references to methods that match their signature.
    D. Once a delegate is assigned a method, it cannot be changed.

Mini Quiz Answers

1. A
2. A
3. A
4. B
5. C

EVENTS

Events allow classes to notify other classes when something occurs. This feature is particularly useful in Graphical User Interfaces (GUI) applications, where events can signify user interactions like button clicks.

An event is defined inside a class using the *event* keyword. The delegate type for the event specifies the method signature of the event handlers that can be attached to the event. A commonly used delegate for events is *EventHandler*, which returns void and takes two parameters: an *object* (the sender) and an *EventArgs* object (providing event data).

Example: Define an Event

```
public event EventHandler WelcomeChanged; // Define the event
```

Before raising an event, it's good practice to check if any event handlers are attached to it. Methods that raise events typically begin with the word "On".

Example: Raise an Event

```
public void OnWelcomeChanged()
{
        WelcomeChanged?.Invoke(this, EventArgs.Empty);
}
```

In the following example, changing the value of *TheMessage* triggers the *OnWelcomeChanged* method, thus raising the event.

Example: Trigger an Event

```
private string theMessage;
public string TheMessage
{
        get { return theMessage; }
        set
        {
                theMessage = $"Hello, {value}";
                OnWelcomeChanged(); // Trigger the event when the property changes
        }
}
```

The method below shows how to handle an event. The signature of this method must match the delegate used for the event (*EventHandler* in this case).

Example: Handle an Event

```
public void HandleWelcomeChanged(object sender, EventArgs eventArgs)
{
        Console.WriteLine("The welcome message has changed!!");
}
```

To attach an event handler to an event, the *+=* operator is used. Multiple event handlers can be attached to a single event.

Example: Attach an Event Handler

```
welcomeMessage.WelcomeChanged += welcomeMessage.HandleWelcomeChanged;
```

Full Example: Using Events

```csharp
class Greetings
{
        private string theMessage;
        public string TheMessage
        {
                get { return theMessage; }
                set
                {
                        theMessage = $"Hello, {value}";
                        OnWelcomeChanged(); // Call OnWelcomeChanged when the value changes
                }
        }

        public event EventHandler WelcomeChanged; // Event declaration

        public void OnWelcomeChanged() // Event declaration
        {
                WelcomeChanged?.Invoke(this, EventArgs.Empty); // Raise the event
        }

        public void HandleWelcomeChanged(object sender, EventArgs eventArgs)
        {
                Console.WriteLine("The welcome message has changed!!");
        }
}

// Usage
Greetings welcomeMessage = new();

// Attach event handler
welcomeMessage.WelcomeChanged += welcomeMessage.HandleWelcomeChanged;

// Trigger the event
welcomeMessage.TheMessage = "Adam";
Console.WriteLine(welcomeMessage.TheMessage);
```

Mini Quiz

1. Events notify other classes when something occurs.

    A. True
    B. False

2. The "+=" operator attaches an event handler to an event.

    A. True
    B. False

3. What is the role of the EventHandler delegate in event handling?

    A. Defines the method signature for event handlers
    B. Automatically raises events
    C. Handles the event itself
    D. None of the above

4. Which method naming convention is commonly used for methods that raise events?

    A. Start with "Raise"
    B. Start with "On"
    C. Start with "Handle"
    D. Start with "Trigger"

5. Can multiple event handlers be attached to a single event?

    A. True
    B. False

Mini Quiz Answers

1. A
2. A
3. A
4. B
5. A

LAMBDAS

A **lambda** expression is essentially an anonymous method, characterized by concise syntax. It's written as a shorthand method and used directly where needed, particularly useful for small, single-use methods. The lambda operator, =>, also known as the "goes to" operator, divides the expression into two parts: the left side (parameter list) and the right side (lambda body).

Example: Lambda Expression

```
Func<int, int> addFive = x => x + 5;
```

C# 12 introduced the ability to specify default values for parameters in lambda expressions. This feature enhances the versatility of lambda expressions, allowing them to be more flexible and aligning their syntax with methods and constructors that support default parameters.

Example: Lambda Expression with Default Values

```
Func<int, int, int> add = (x, y = 1) => x + y;
```

In this example, the lambda expression *add* can be invoked with one or two arguments. If the second argument is omitted, it defaults to 1.

Example: Lambda Using a Delegate

```
Func<int, int> addFive = x => x + 5;
Console.WriteLine(addFive(2)); // Output: 7
```

In this example, *Func<int, int>* is a built-in delegate type that takes an integer as input and returns an integer.

Full Example: Lambdas and Lists

```csharp
List<int> numbers = new() { 5, 3, 4, 5, 6, 7 };

// Finds all instances of 5 in the list
List<int> numberFives = numbers.FindAll(x => x == 5);
Console.WriteLine($"There are {numberFives.Count} 5's in the list");

// Finds all odd numbers in the list
List<int> oddNumbers = numbers.FindAll(x => (x % 2) != 0);
Console.WriteLine($"There are {oddNumbers.Count} Odd numbers in the list");
```

Lambda expressions can also be used in various expression-bodied members that are a single expression. This is an elegant way to simplify methods or properties that consist of only one expression.

Full Example: Expression-bodied Members with Lambda Expression Syntax

```csharp
Console.WriteLine(SquareNumber1(5)); // Output: 25
Console.WriteLine(SquareNumber2(5)); // Output: 25

// Regular method
static int SquareNumber1(int number)
{
        return number * number;
}

// Lambda expression syntax for the same method
static int SquareNumber2(int number) => number * number;
```

Mini Quiz

1. The following is a lambda operator "<=".

    A. True
    B. False

2. The lambda operator separates the expression into two parts.

    A. True
    B. False

3. The following code would output 7.

```
Console.WriteLine(AMethod(2));
static int AMethod(int number) => number + number + number + 1;
```

    A. True
    B. False

4. What will the following lambda expression find in a list of integers?

```
numbers.FindAll(x => (x % 2) != 0);
```

    A. All even numbers
    B. All odd numbers
    C. All prime numbers
    D. Numbers greater than 2

Mini Quiz Answers

1. B
2. A
3. A
4. B

THREADS

Threads allow for running *multiple* sections of code simultaneously, enabling code execution on multiple processors and potentially boosting performance.

To use threads, you typically include the *System.Threading* namespace. However, with C# 10 and later versions, Implicit Usings are introduced, automatically including common namespaces like *System.Threading*, so explicit declaration might not be necessary.

The *Thread* class allows for creating and managing threads. It's important to note that the *Thread* constructor requires a delegate that points to a method returning *void*.

Example: Create a Thread Object

```
Thread aThread = new(CountTo200);
```

To start a thread, you use the Start method. This method can be invoked with zero or one argument, depending on the thread method's requirements.

Example: Start a Thread

```
aThread.Start();    // 0 parameters
bThread.Start(45); // 1 parameter
```

Full Example: Thread with No Parameters

```
Thread aThread = new(CountTo200);
Thread bThread = new(CountTo200);
aThread.Start();
bThread.Start();

static void CountTo200()
{
        for (int i = 1; i <= 200; i++)
        {
                Console.WriteLine(i);
        }
}
```

In this example, two threads execute the *CountTo200* method concurrently. The output will interleave because both threads run simultaneously, and their execution order is not guaranteed.

The *Join* method is used to make one thread wait for another to complete. This can be useful for synchronizing threads.

Example: Join Method

```
aThread.Join();
```

Full Example: Using Join

```
Thread aThread = new(CountTo200);
Thread bThread = new(CountTo200);
aThread.Start();
aThread.Join(); // Waits for aThread to complete
bThread.Start();
bThread.Join(); // Waits for bThread to complete

static void CountTo200()
{
        for (int i = 1; i <= 200; i++)
        {
                Console.WriteLine(i);
        }
}
```

Threads can also be started with parameters. The parameter passed to the *Start* method must be of type object and can be cast to the appropriate type within the thread method.

Full Example: Thread – One Parameter

```
Thread aThread = new(CountTo);
aThread.Start(45); // Start with an integer parameter

static void CountTo(object count)
{
        for (int i = 1; i <= (int)count; i++)
        {
                Console.WriteLine(i);
        }
}
```

When using threads, it's important to consider thread safety, especially when accessing shared resources. Synchronizing access to shared data is crucial to prevent race conditions and ensure data integrity.

ACTIVITY: THREADS

Activity: This activity is designed to provide hands-on experience with threading. You'll create a Console Application named "ThreadsApp" that demonstrates the use of multiple threads and their interaction.

1. **Create Three Separate Threads**: Initialize three different threads in your application.

2. **Create a Counting Method**: Implement a method named *CountToHundred* that counts to 100. This method should also display the current count along with the thread's name or ID that is executing it.

3. **Demonstrate Thread Start and Execution**: Each thread should start the *CountToHundred* method.

Expected Outcome:

The console output should display the count from 1 to 100 for each thread, with the thread identifier indicating which thread is currently executing. Due to the nature of threading, the numbers might not be displayed in sequence, and thread executions may interleave.

Example output format (actual results will vary):

```
Thread 1: 1
Thread 2: 1
Thread 1: 2
Thread 3: 1
...
```

Need help with the solution? https://www.unQbd.com/Solutions/CSharp7th/Threads

ASYNCHRONOUS

Asynchronous programming is pivotal in enhancing application responsiveness by executing non-blocking operations, thereby preventing bottlenecks. The essence of asynchronous programming is encapsulated in two keywords: **async** and **await**.

Async Methods: Marking a method with the *async* keyword enables it to utilize the *await* keyword. When *await* is encountered, the program can continue with other tasks, while the awaited operation completes in the background. Asynchronous methods typically return **void**, **Task**, or **Task<TResult>**, with the latter two being preferable for better control and error handling. The naming convention for async methods often includes appending "Async" to their names.

Full Example: Async Void Method

```csharp
static async void FirstMethodAsync()
{
        Console.WriteLine("Task Started");
        await Task.Delay(3000); // Simulates a 3-second delay
        Console.WriteLine("Task Finished");
}
```

It's important to note that *async void* methods are generally used for event handlers. In other contexts, **async Task** is preferred due to better error handling and control flow.

Returning Tasks: More commonly, async methods return a *Task* or *Task<TResult>*. *Task* is used when there's no return value, and *Task<TResult>* when a result is expected. This allows the method to be awaited in other async methods, providing better control over the operation.

Full Example: Async Task Method

```csharp
static async Task SecondMethodAsync()
{
        await Task.Delay(3000); // Simulates a 3-second delay
        Console.WriteLine("Second Task Finished");
}
```

Async Methods with Return Values: When an async method needs to return a value, *Task<TResult>* is used. The result of the awaited task can then be processed further.

Full Example: Async Task<TResult> Method

```
static async Task<string> SecondMethodAsync()
{
        await Task.Delay(3000); // Simulates a 3-second delay
        return "Second Task Finished";
}
```

Best Practices and Exception Handling: When using async/await, it's crucial to adhere to best practices like avoiding *async void* (except for event handlers), using *async Task* for better testability and error handling, and being aware of potential deadlocks, especially in UI applications. Additionally, understanding how exceptions are handled in async methods (rethrown upon awaiting the task) is important for robust error management.

MINI QUIZ: ASYNCHRONOUS

Mini Quiz

1. Asynchronous programing helps reduce the chance of a program responsiveness from "freezing".

    A. True

    B. False

2. The naming convention for an async method is to append them with an "async" prefix.

    A. True

    B. False

3. If the async modifier is used, the await operator also has to be used.

    A. True

    B. False

4. Async methods must have a return type of Task, Task<T>, or void.

    A. True

    B. False

5. Which of the following is a recommended practice for async methods?

    A. Always use async void

    B. Prefer async Task or async Task<T> over async void

    C. Avoid using await within async methods

    D. Use async methods only for event handlers

Mini Quiz Answers

1. A

2. B – Append suffix Async with not prefix

3. A

4. A

5. B

QUERY EXPRESSIONS: LINQ – QUERY SYNTAX

LINQ (Language Integrated Query) is a powerful feature for querying collections of data. LINQ provides two syntaxes: query syntax (covered here) and method syntax. Query syntax is similar to SQL and is often more readable for complex queries.

To use LINQ, ensure *System.Linq* is included at the top of your code file. Note that C# 10 and later may implicitly include this namespace.

The query begins with a *'from'* clause, which defines the data source and a range variable for the query.

Example: "From" Clause

```
from o in students
```

The *'select'* clause specifies the elements to select from the query, either as partial or complete objects.

Example: "Select" Clause

```
select o;
```

The *'where'* clause is used to apply a filter to the query based on specified conditions.

Example: "Where" Clause

```
where o.Grade > 90
```

The results from a LINQ query are always output as *IEnumerable<T>* and can be converted to a list or array using *ToList()* or *ToArray()*.

Example: Full Expression Using "Where" Clause

```
IEnumerable<StudentInfo> aStudents = from o in students
                                     where o.Grade > 90
                                     select o;
```

The *'let'* clause creates a derived variable for use within the query, simplifying complex operations.

Example: "Let" Clause

```
let averageGrade = (o.Grade1 + o.Grade2) / 2
```

The *'join'* clause joins two collections based on a matching condition, typically used for correlating data from different sources.

Example: "Join" Clause

```
join b in books on o.StudentID equals b.StudentID
```

The *'orderby'* clause sorts the results of the query in descending order.

Example: "OrderBy" Clause

```
orderby o.Name descending
```

Example: Full Expression Using "OrderBy" Clause

```
IEnumerable<StudentInfo> aStudents = from o in students
                        orderby o.Name // Ascending by default
                        select o;
```

The *'group'* clause bundles elements into groups based on a specified key, useful for categorizing data.

Example: "Group" Clause

```
group o by o.BookName;
```

The following comprehensive example demonstrates various LINQ queries.

Full Example: Query Expressions

```csharp
class StudentInfo
{
        public int StudentID { get; set; }
        public string Name { get; set; }
        public int Grade1 { get; set; }
        public int Grade2 { get; set; }
}

class BookInfo
{
        public int StudentID { get; set; } = 0;
        public string BookName { get; set; }
}

// Create sample data for students and books
List<StudentInfo> students = new()
{
        new StudentInfo {StudentID = 1, Name = "Jonathan", Grade1 = 95, Grade2 = 90},
        new StudentInfo {StudentID = 2, Name = "Maria", Grade1 = 92, Grade2 = 85},
        new StudentInfo {StudentID = 3, Name = "Marcos", Grade1 = 81, Grade2 = 91}
};

List<BookInfo> books = new()
{
        new BookInfo {StudentID = 1, BookName = "C# Fundamentals"},
        new BookInfo {StudentID = 1, BookName = "Microsoft Magazine"},
        new BookInfo {StudentID = 2, BookName = "C# Fundamentals"}
};

// Minimal query expression
IEnumerable<StudentInfo> students1 = from o in students select o;

// Query specifying items with Grade1 greater than 90
IEnumerable<StudentInfo> students2 = from o in students where o.Grade1 > 90  select o;

// Display grades greater than 90
foreach (var student in students2)
{
        Console.WriteLine($"Name: {student.Name} Grade: {student.Grade1}");
}



// OrderBy sorts all items in a collection
```

```csharp
IEnumerable<StudentInfo> students3 = from o in students
                                     orderby o.Name
                                     select o;

// Groups bundle elements into groups based on the information specified
var bookGroups = from o in books
                 group o by o.BookName into g
                 select g;

// Display information about the groups
foreach (var group in bookGroups)
{
        Console.WriteLine($"Group Key: {group.Key}");
        foreach (var book in group)
        {
                Console.WriteLine($"Book: {book.BookName}, StudentID: {book.StudentID}");
        }
        Console.WriteLine();
}
```

QUERY EXPRESSIONS: LINQ – METHOD CALL SYNTAX

LINQ **method call syntax**, utilizing lambda expressions, provides an alternative to the query syntax covered in the previous section. This syntax is often more concise and can be preferable for simpler queries or when working with certain LINQ methods.

Lambda expressions are anonymous functions that provide a concise way to represent an anonymous method. They are especially useful in LINQ method call syntax for specifying conditions and transformations.

Example: "Where" Clause

```
// Previous query syntax
IEnumerable<StudentInfo> querySyntaxStudents = from o in students
                                               where o.Grade1 > 90
                                               select o;
// Method call syntax
IEnumerable<StudentInfo> methodSyntaxStudents = students.Where(o => o.Grade1 > 90);
```

This example demonstrates how to filter a collection using the *Where* clause.

Example: "Where" and "Select" Clause

```
// Previous query syntax
IEnumerable<string> querySyntaxNames = from o in students
                                       where o.Grade1 > 90
                                       select o.Name;
// Method call syntax
IEnumerable<string> methodSyntaxNames = students.Where(o => o.Grade1 > 90).Select(o => o.Name);
```

Here, the *Where* and Select clauses are combined to filter and project data.

Example: "OrderBy" and "Select" Clause

```
// Previous query syntax
IEnumerable<string> queryOrderedNames = from o in students
                                        orderby o.Name
                                        select o.Name;
// Method call syntax
IEnumerable<string> methodOrderedNames = students.OrderBy(o => o.Name).Select(o => o.Name);
```

Method call syntax is particularly useful for chaining multiple LINQ operations in a single expression. It offers the flexibility and power of LINQ in a compact form, ideal for many scenarios in data querying and manipulation.

WALKTHROUGH: CREATING A DATABASE WITH ENTITY FRAMEWORK

Databases store collections of information in an organized way, allowing for easy data manipulation. In this chapter, we will create a local **SQL** database for **CRUD** (Create, Read, Update, Delete) operations using Entity Framework.

Walkthrough: Creating a Database

1. **Create a Console Application:** Start by creating a .NET Console Application in Visual Studio and naming it "StudentDB".

2. **Install Entity Framework:** Make sure Entity Framework and its dependencies are installed. In Visual Studio, right-click on the "StudentDB" project and select "Manage NuGet Packages". Install the following packages if they are not already installed:

- Microsoft.EntityFrameworkCore

- Microsoft.EntityFrameworkCore.Tools

- Microsoft.EntityFrameworkCore.SqlServer

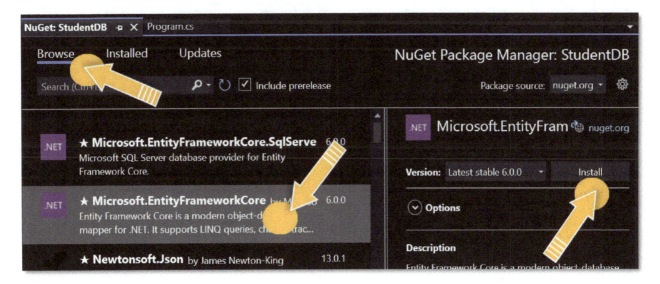

3. Setup Model and Context:

A. Create the Model:

Create a *"People"* folder in the project and add a *Student* class to define the model. In C# 13, we use a **primary constructor** for a cleaner definition:

```csharp
namespace StudentDB.People
{
        class Student
        {
                public int Id { get; } = id;
                public string Name { get; } = name;
                public int Grade { get; } = grade;
        }
}
```

B. Setup the Database Context:

Create a *"Data"* folder in the project, and add a *StudentDBContext* class to manage the database connection, inheriting from *DbContext*.

```csharp
using  Microsoft.EntityFrameworkCore;
using StudentDB.People;

namespace StudentDB.Data
{
internal class StudentDBContext : DbContext
{
public StudentDBContext(DbContextOptions<StudentDBContext> options) : base(options)
{
}
        public DbSet<Student> Students { get; set; }

        // Database connection
        protected override void OnConfiguring(DbContextOptionsBuilder optionsBuilder)
        {
                if (!optionsBuilder.IsConfigured)
                {
optionsBuilder.UseSqlServer(@"Server=(localdb)\MSSQLLocalDB;Database=StudentDatabase;Trusted_Connection=True;");
                }
        }
}
}
```

4. Implement Migrations:

Use migrations to synchronize the database schema with the models. In the Package Manager Console (Tools -> NuGet Package Manager -> Package Manager Console):

- Run *Add-Migration InitialMigration* to scaffold the initial tables.
- Execute *Update-Database* to create the database.

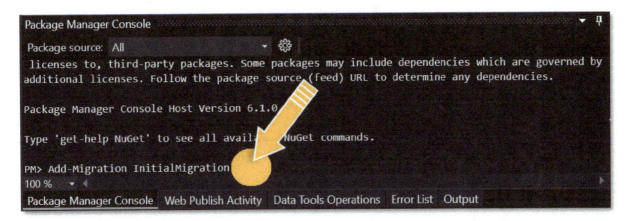

5. View the Database:

Use SQL Server Object Explorer in Visual Studio to view *StudentDatabase*. Navigate to *dbo.Students -> View Data to* check the table.

Alternatively, if you're using Visual Studio Code or a different IDE, you can connect to the database using SQL Server Management Studio (SSMS) to explore its tables.

6. Data Entry Test:

Initially, test data entry directly into the database table. Proper data manipulation using code will be covered in the next section.

DATABASE OPERATIONS USING ENTITY FRAMEWORK

This section continues from the "Creating a Database with Entity Framework" and demonstrates how to perform various CRUD operations using Entity Framework.

Adding Items to a Database

Include the following code in the *Main* method of *Program.cs to add items to the database*. Ensure that *using StudentDB.Data;* and *using StudentDB.People;* are added at the top.

Example: Adding Items to a Database

```
using (var db = new StudentDBContext())
{
        db.Students.AddRange(
                new Student { 1, "Wyatt", 95 },
                new Student { 2, "Kristen", 98 }
        );
        await db.SaveChangesAsync();
}
```

TIP - **Use Async Methods:** Always prefer using await db.SaveChangesAsync() to enhance performance, especially in applications where responsiveness matters (e.g., web applications).

Displaying Each Entry in a Database Table

To loop through and display each entry in a database table:

Example: Display Results

```
using (var db = new StudentDBContext())
{
        foreach (var student in db.Students)
        {
                Console.WriteLine($"Name: {student.Name} Grade: {student.Grade}");
        }
}
```

Filtering Results Using the *Where* Clause

Example: "Where" Query and Display Results

```
using (var db = new StudentDBContext())
{
        var studentInfo = db.Students.Where(student => student.Name == "Wyatt");

        foreach (var student in studentInfo)
        {
                Console.WriteLine($"Name: {student.Name} Grade: {student.Grade}");
        }
}
```

Use **relational pattern matching** to simplify complex filtering conditions:

```
var topStudents = db.Students.Where(student => student.Grade is > 90);
```

Partial String Matching Using *Contains*

Example: Using Contains

```
using (var db = new StudentDBContext())
{
        var query = db.Students.Where(student => student.Name.Contains("Ale"));
}
```

Sorting Results Using *OrderBy*

Example: Using OrderBy

```
using (var db = new StudentDBContext())
{
        var query = db.Students.OrderBy(student => student.Name);
}
```

There are built in aggregate functions such as **Average**, **Sum**, **Max**, and **Min**.

Example: Aggregate Functions

```
using (var db = new StudentDBContext())
{
        var maxGrade = db.Students.Max(student => student.Age);
        Console.WriteLine($"Highest Grade: {maxGrade}");
}
```

Removing Items from a Table

To remove items from a table, use **RemoveRange** or **Remove**. After removing the items, **SaveChangesAsync** must be called to update the database.

Example: Removing Items

```
using (var db = new StudentDBContext())
{
        db.Students.RemoveRange(db.Students.Where(student => student.Name == "Wyatt"));
        await db.SaveChangesAsync();
}
```

Selecting Specific Columns for Improved Performance

Example: Select Specific Columns

```
using (var db = new StudentDBContext())
{
        var query = db.Students.Select(student => new { student.Name });
}
```

Example: "Where" and "Select" Multiple Columns

```
using (var db = new StudentDBContext())
{
   var query = db.Students
                .Where(s => student.Name == "Bill")
                .Select(s => new { student.Name, student.Grade });
}
```

Retrieving Specific Entries

Methods like **Single**, **SingleOrDefault**, **First**, and **FirstOrDefault** are used to retrieve specific entries:

- **Single**: Use when there is exactly one result. An exception will be thrown if no results or multiple results are returned.
- **SingleOrDefault:** Similar to *Single*, but returns *null* if no results are found.
- **First:** Use to return the first result. An exception will be thrown if no results are found.
- **FirstOrDefault** similar to *First*, but returns *null* if no results are found.

Example: Single, SingleOrDefault, First, FirstOrDefault

```
using (var db = new StudentDBContext())
{
        try
        {
        var querySingle = db.Students.Single(student => student.Name == "Wyatt");
        var querySingleOrDefault = db.Students.SingleOrDefault(student => student.Name == "Wyatt");
        var queryFirst = db.Students.First(student => student.Name == "Wyatt");
        var queryFirstOrDefault = db.Students.FirstOrDefault(student => student.Name == "Wyatt");

        if (querySingleOrDefault == null)
        {
        Console.WriteLine("Student not found.");
        }
        }
}
```

Combining Data from Two Tables Using *join*

To combine data from two tables, use the *join* clause

Example: Joining Tables

```csharp
using (var db = new StudentDBContext())
{
        var query = from student in db.Students    // Database Table 1
                    join other in db.AnotherTable // Database Table 2
                    on student.ID equals other.StudentID
                    select new { student.Name, student.Grade, other.Age };

        foreach (var item in query)
        {
                Console.WriteLine($"Name: {item.Name} Grade: {item.Grade} Age: {item.Age}");
        }
}
```

FINAL THOUGHT

Congratulations on completing your journey through this C# programming guide! With the knowledge and skills you've gained, you are well-prepared to build a wide variety of applications. The journey of learning and development, however, is ongoing.

Where to Go from Here:

- **Explore Further Resources**: Continue expanding your knowledge with more programming books and resources. A great place to start is unQbd.com, which offers a range of materials for deepening your programming understanding.

- **Engage in Practical Projects**: The best way to sharpen your skills is through practice. Think of a personal project that excites you, be it a game, an application, or a tool, and start building it. This hands-on experience is invaluable.

- **Join Online Communities**: Connect with other developers by participating in online forums and communities. Platforms like Stack Overflow, GitHub, or dedicated C# forums can be excellent for gaining insights, asking questions, and collaborating on projects.

- **Dive into Advanced Topics**: Challenge yourself with more advanced C# topics and technologies. Whether it's mastering asynchronous programming, exploring .NET Core for cross-platform development, or delving into microservices, there's always more to learn.

- **Contribute to Open Source Projects**: Look for open-source projects on platforms like GitHub that align with your interests. Contributing to these projects can enhance your coding skills and expand your professional network.

- **Keep Up-to-Date with Industry Trends**: The tech world is constantly evolving. Stay informed about the latest developments in C# and .NET to keep your skills relevant and cutting-edge.

- **Teach and Share Your Knowledge**: Consider teaching what you've learned to others. Whether through blogging, creating tutorials, or mentoring, teaching can reinforce your own understanding and benefit the wider community.

Remember, your growth as a programmer is a continuous journey. Every challenge you tackle, every line of code you write, and every project you complete contributes to your experience and expertise. Embrace the process, stay curious, and keep building. The world of coding awaits!